Oil Spills

Other Books in the Current Controversies Series

Oil Spills

Tamara Thompson, Book Editor

GREENHAVEN PRESS
A part of Gale, Cengage Learning

GALE
CENGAGE Learning·

Detroit • New York • San Francisco • New Haven, Conn • Waterville, Maine • London

Elizabeth Des Chenes, *Director, Content Strategy*
Cynthia Sanner, *Publisher*
Douglas Dentino, *Manager, New Product*

© 2014 Greenhaven Press, a part of Gale, Cengage Learning

WCN: 01-100-101

LIBRARY OF CONGRESS CATALOGING-IN-PUBLICATION DATA

Oil spills / Tamara Thompson, book editor.
    p. cm. -- (Current controversies)
  Includes bibliographical references and index.
    ISBN 978-0-7377-6880-0 (hardback) -- ISBN 978-0-7377-6881-7 (paperback)
  1. Oil spills. 2. Petroleum industry and trade--Accidents. I. Thompson, Tamara.
  TD427.P4O3884 2014
  363.738'2--dc23
                                                                    2013028043

Printed in the United States of America
1 2 3 4 5 6 7 18 17 16 15 14

Contents

Chapter 1: How Do Oil Spills Happen?

Andrea Thompson

Oil spills can happen in a variety of different ways at
various stages of the oil extraction, transportation, and
refining processes. The type of oil that is spilled and
where the spill happens determine how fast it spreads
and how much environmental impact it has.

Charles H. Peterson et al.

Because the 2010 *Deepwater Horizon* well blowout in the
Gulf of Mexico happened at such an unprecedented
depth—nearly 5,000 feet—both the oil and the clean-up
equipment behaved differently and the spill could not be
contained in the usual ways. Never before had a spill
happened in such an extreme environment, and it revealed the unique risks involved with deepwater drilling
and the failure of response systems that were based on
inadequate models.

Keith Schneider

The type of oil extracted from tar sands is called diluted
bitumen, or DilBit for short. It is more dangerous to
transport than regular crude oil because it is highly
acidic, abrasive, and corrosive, and must be diluted and
moved under high pressure through steel pipelines. These
characteristics can weaken the pipelines and increase the
risk of a spill, such as the one that occurred in Michigan
in 2010.

During the first Gulf War in 1991, Iraqi forces intentionally opened valves at an oil terminal and dumped oil
from several tankers, deliberately spilling several million
barrels into the Persian Gulf. The Iraqis also set more
than five hundred oil wells on fire in Kuwait, and it took
nearly a year to extinguish and recap them all. More than
twenty years later the environmental consequences of the
world's biggest oil spill still remain.

Chapter 2: Is the Risk of a Spill Worth Drilling for Oil?

Americans are about evenly divided on the question of
whether energy production or environmental protection
should be prioritized in public policy. A 2012 Gallup poll
found that Republicans are more likely to prioritize energy development than they have been in the past, while
Democrats have consistently prioritized environmental
concerns.

Yes: The Risk of a Spill Is Worth Drilling for Oil

The cost of cleaning up an oil spill is a necessary tradeoff for the conveniences of modern life. When one weighs
the economic and environmental costs of a spill, it is
clear that the benefits of producing offshore oil greatly
outweigh the impacts. Offshore drilling continues to be a
reasonable risk.

Despite recent spills and concerns about safety, more pipelines will soon be carrying heavy oil from tar sands than ever before. That is because the large supply of tar sands oil from Canada, along with oil from the Bakken formation in North Dakota, could make North America self-sufficient in oil production within fifteen years. Transporting all this oil by pipeline remains the best way for that to become a reality.

No: The Risk of a Spill Is Not Worth Drilling for Oil

Chapter 3: Is the Oil Industry Prepared to Handle Major Oil Spills?

Foreword

By definition, controversies are "discussions of questions in which opposing opinions clash" (*Webster's Twentieth Century Dictionary Unabridged*). Few would deny that controversies are a pervasive part of the human condition and exist on virtually every level of human enterprise. Controversies transpire between individuals and among groups, within nations and between nations. Controversies supply the grist necessary for progress by providing challenges and challengers to the status quo. They also create atmospheres where strife and warfare can flourish. A world without controversies would be a peaceful world; but it also would be, by and large, static and prosaic.

The Series' Purpose

The purpose of the Current Controversies series is to explore many of the social, political, and economic controversies dominating the national and international scenes today. Titles selected for inclusion in the series are highly focused and specific. For example, from the larger category of criminal justice, Current Controversies deals with specific topics such as police brutality, gun control, white collar crime, and others. The debates in Current Controversies also are presented in a useful, timeless fashion. Articles and book excerpts included in each title are selected if they contribute valuable, long-range ideas to the overall debate. And wherever possible, current information is enhanced with historical documents and other relevant materials. Thus, while individual titles are current in focus, every effort is made to ensure that they will not become quickly outdated. Books in the Current Controversies series will remain important resources for librarians, teachers, and students for many years.

In addition to keeping the titles focused and specific, great care is taken in the editorial format of each book in the series. Book introductions and chapter prefaces are offered to provide background material for readers. Chapters are organized around several key questions that are answered with diverse opinions representing all points on the political spectrum. Materials in each chapter include opinions in which authors clearly disagree as well as alternative opinions in which authors may agree on a broader issue but disagree on the possible solutions. In this way, the content of each volume in Current Controversies mirrors the mosaic of opinions encountered in society. Readers will quickly realize that there are many viable answers to these complex issues. By questioning each author's conclusions, students and casual readers can begin to develop the critical thinking skills so important to evaluating opinionated material.

Current Controversies is also ideal for controlled research. Each anthology in the series is composed of primary sources taken from a wide gamut of informational categories including periodicals, newspapers, books, US and foreign government documents, and the publications of private and public organizations. Readers will find factual support for reports, debates, and research papers covering all areas of important issues. In addition, an annotated table of contents, an index, a book and periodical bibliography, and a list of organizations to contact are included in each book to expedite further research.

Perhaps more than ever before in history, people are confronted with diverse and contradictory information. During the Persian Gulf War, for example, the public was not only treated to minute-to-minute coverage of the war, it was also inundated with critiques of the coverage and countless analyses of the factors motivating US involvement. Being able to sort through the plethora of opinions accompanying today's major issues, and to draw one's own conclusions, can be a complicated and frustrating struggle. It is the editors' hope that Current Controversies will help readers with this struggle.

Introduction

"The Gulf oil spill in 2010 brought the dual realities of oil production into sharp focus for the American public and served as a wake-up call for both the environmental movement and the oil industry in different ways."

It is impossible to talk about oil spills without talking about economics and politics. Oil production in the United States is inextricably linked to the national economy, the country's energy security, and to both foreign and domestic policy. It is linked to the stock market, to corporate shareholders, to millions of American jobs, to the price of gasoline, and to the cost of running a business or buying a loaf of bread. It is linked to US independence from foreign oil; to the demand for construction, transportation, and manufacturing; and to the further development of the country's energy infrastructure. It is linked to the nation's economic recovery and to a new oil boom in North Dakota that has revitalized an entire region. It is linked to the future availability of cheap oil and to nothing less than the continuance of the American way of life.

Because oil production is linked to all of these things in such deep and complex ways, the potential for spills—even devastating ones like the *Deepwater Horizon* well blowout that spewed some 210 million gallons of crude into the Gulf of Mexico over three months in 2010—is considered by many to be an unfortunate but unavoidable fact of modern life. The benefits of oil are so powerful—and the economic and political connections so pervasive—that it can be difficult to reconcile that reality with another equally powerful one: oil can spill in massive quantities from tankers, pipelines, and wells—

and when it does, it becomes inextricably linked to other things entirely. It becomes linked to the permanent fouling of pristine environments and complex ecosystems and to the deaths of thousands of birds and other creatures. It becomes linked to massive die-offs of marine life and coral, to genetic deformities in fish and crabs, and to the collapse of nature-based economies, such as fishing and tourism. It becomes linked to public health concerns over air and water quality, cancer, birth defects, and debilitating health conditions from exposure to oil and toxic cleanup materials. It becomes linked to mental health problems, neurological disorders, and to chemicals that linger in the environment and food chain for generations, causing long-term effects on both humans and marine life.

As the largest accidental off-shore oil spill in the world and the biggest environmental disaster in US history, the Gulf oil spill in 2010 brought the dual realities of oil production into sharp focus for the American public and served as a wake-up call for both the environmental movement and the oil industry in different ways.

For environmental groups, the Gulf spill became a touch-stone for their campaigns on a variety of clean-energy issues, from opposing drilling in the Arctic National Wildlife Refuge and construction of the Keystone XL Pipeline (which would carry heavy tar sands oil from Canada to US Gulf Coast refineries), to demanding alternative energy solutions and arguing that an economy based on dirty fossil fuels is unsustainable and irresponsible at its very core. The Gulf spill awakened a whole new generation of Americans to environmental activism, and the result of that new awareness is reflected in the numbers; nearly three years after the spill, an estimated fifty thousand people marched from the Washington Monument to the White House on February 17, 2013, for the "Forward on Climate Rally," the largest environmental protest in US history. The event's primary focus was to oppose the Keystone XL Pipeline project.

The same month, British Petroleum (BP)—the leaseholder on the Macondo sea-floor well being serviced by Transocean Ltd's ill-fated *Deepwater Horizon* drilling rig—answered another summons in its own continuing wake-up call. BP, Transocean, and other companies involved in the Macondo well began standing trial in federal court to determine the companies' financial liabilities for the Gulf spill disaster. The civil trial, which began February 25, 2013, focuses on violations of the Clean Water Act and whether each company's actions constituted willful misconduct and/or gross negligence. If found to be so, the judgment could climb as high as $17.6 billion, which would be the largest environmental penalty in US history.

In November 2012, BP agreed to an unprecedented criminal judgment of $4.5 billion, pleading guilty to eleven counts of felony manslaughter for the workers killed in the incident as well as to one count of obstruction of Congress and various other charges. BP previously agreed to a $7.8 billion settlement of medical and economic claims, and thousands of private lawsuits against the oil giant are still pending. To date, BP has racked up more than $24 billion in spill-related expenses (including cleanup), and the company expects to eventually spend about $42 billion to finalize its total liability. Transocean Ltd., which owned and operated *Deepwater Horizon* under the drilling contract with BP, agreed in February 2013 to settle criminal charges against it for $400 million and to settle a civil suit for $1 billion; Transocean remains one of the co-defendants in the ongoing Clean Water Act federal civil trial by the Justice Department.

To say that the oil industry has been served notice that it will be held liable for the consequences of its actions would be an understatement. The industry has responded to the *Deepwater Horizon* catastrophe by shouldering liability, strengthening its safety standards, and improving spill response planning to reassure regulatory bodies and a nervous public that it can be a responsible environmental steward. But at the same time, it pushes to expand drilling operations into ever more extreme and unpredictable environments, such as the Arctic, that entail new technical challenges and new risks for devastating spills.

The authors in *Current Controversies: Oil Spills* represent a wide range of viewpoints on key questions about how oil spills happen, whether the oil industry is sufficiently regulated, whether oil companies are prepared to clean up major spills, and whether the risk of a spill is worth drilling for oil in the first place.

CHAPTER 1

How Do Oil Spills Happen?

Overview: The Science and History Behind Oil Spills

Andrea Thompson

Andrea Thompson is a senior writer for LiveScience, a science news website that syndicates its stories and editorial commentary to major news outlets around the world.

The explosion and sinking of an oil rig in the middle of the Gulf of Mexico on [April 20, 2010] has created a potentially serious environmental situation, though experts are not sure how bad it might be. That all depends on whether the oil from the rig's well spills and where it goes.

From what we do know, here are answers to some common questions about oil spills:

Why do so many oil spills happen?

In brief, because there are a lot of tricky steps to get oil from inside the Earth to inside, say, your gas tank. Oil spills can be caused by the accidental or intentional release of any form of petroleum during any point in the oil production process, from drilling, refining, or storing to transporting. Oil can be spilled when a pipeline breaks, ships collide or are grounded (as happened earlier this month along the Great Barrier Reef), underground storage tanks leak, or in the current case, when an oil rig explodes or is damaged.

Some oil was spilled when the *Deepwater Horizon* rig first burst into flames on April 20 in the Gulf, injuring crew members and sending a billowing plume of black smoke into the sky that could be seen by satellite.

The oil rig, located about 51 miles (82 kilometers) southeast of Venice, La., then sank into the Gulf waters Thursday morning, creating concern that more oil could spill.

Oil spills can also happen naturally: Oil is released into the ocean from natural oil seeps on the seafloor. The best known such seep is Coal Oil Point along the California coast where an estimated 2,000 to 3,000 gallons (7,570 to 11,400 liters) of crude oil is released each day.

The Impacts of a Spill

How fast does oil in a spill spread?

Oil can spread very rapidly unless it is quickly contained by a boom (a large floating barrier that can round up and lift the oil out of the water) or other mechanism.

The lighter the oil is, the faster it can spread—so gasoline would spread faster than thicker, black oils, such as the crude oil from the *Deepwater Horizon*. But even heavy oil can spread quickly in a major spill, spreading out as thin as a layer of paint on a wall in just a few hours, according to the U.S. National Oceanic and Atmospheric Administration (NOAA). . . .

How do oil spills impact wildlife?

Oil slicks, like the one currently floating in the Gulf, affect wildlife by coating their bodies in the water-repelling gunk. Since it floats, all sorts of marine animals, even birds, can take a hit. And fish sometimes mistake the floating slick for food and so are attracted to it, according to the Australian Maritime Safety Authority.

Offshore drilling in U.S. territorial waters accounted for 30.2 percent of U.S. oil production in 2009.

When birds' feathers get coated with oil, they lose their ability to trap air and repel water, meaning the animals can't maintain body heat. The result: hypothermia. Marine animals, such as sea otters, which depend on their clean fur coats to stay warm, can also become hypothermic, according to the Oiled Wildlife Care Network.

Currently, the oil rig is currently well offshore, though experts have said any turn in winds and currents could send oil toward coastal wetlands where plenty of animals live. In addition, a pod of sperm whales is known to feed in the area of the oil well where the *Deepwater Horizon* sank, according to news reports.

1.3 million gallons (4.9 million liters) of petroleum are spilled into U.S. waters from vessels and pipelines in a typical year. A major oil spill could easily double that amount.

Oil Spill Statistics

What percentage of U.S. oil comes from offshore rigs?

According to the Minerals Management Service, offshore drilling in U.S. territorial waters accounted for 30.2 percent of U.S. oil production in 2009 (379 million barrels of oil), and 11.4 percent of U.S. natural gas production (1.6 trillion cubic feet or about 12 trillion gallons).

What is crude oil?

Most of the oil products in the United States are made out of crude oil—the rough, unprocessed form of oil. Gasoline, heating oil, petroleum and diesel fuel are all made from crude oil. Depending on the stage of processing, any one of these oils can get spilled into the environment. If the spill happens during the extraction process, crude oil is leaked. However, if the spill occurs after the crude oil has been refined, diesel fuel or petroleum is leaked. If the spill happens when a tanker's fuel supply is punctured, gasoline—another refined crude oil product—would seep into the environment.

What type of oil spill causes the most harm?

Gasoline and diesel fuel molecules are smaller than crude oil molecules. Because of this, gasoline and diesel spills evaporate more quickly. However, these oils are highly toxic to living things, and can kill organisms that breathe in their fumes or absorb these oils through their skin.

The Impacts of Crude Oil

Crude oil and other so-called heavy oils are dangerous in a different way. Although they are less toxic, they are thick and gluey and can smother living creatures. By covering the feathers of birds or the fur of marine mammals, these oils prevent the animals from maintaining their normal body temperatures, leading to death from hypothermia. And these oils don't evaporate, so they can remain in the environment for much longer.

How much oil is spilled into the ocean every year?

According to the U.S. Department of Energy, 1.3 million gallons (4.9 million liters) of petroleum are spilled into U.S. waters from vessels and pipelines in a typical year. A major oil spill could easily double that amount.

Between 1971 and 2000, the U.S. Coast Guard identified more than 250,000 oil spills in U.S. waters, according to a 2002 report from the U.S. Department of the Interior Minerals Management Service.

Approximately 1.7 billion gallons (6.4 billion liters) of oil were lost as a result of tanker incidents from 1970 to 2009, according to International Tanker Owners Pollution Federation Limited, which collects data on oil spills from tankers and other sources.

What is the world's biggest oil spill?

The Persian Gulf oil spill of 1991 is so far the biggest oil spill in the world. As Iraqi troops retreated from Kuwait during the first Gulf War, they opened the valves of oil wells and pipelines, pouring up to 8 million barrels into the Gulf, though estimates on the exact amount of oil spilled vary. This would put this spill at several times the size of the *Exxon Valdez* disaster.

Tankers and Pipelines

How many oil spills are caused by rigs and how many by tankers?

Tanker accidents have accounted for most of the world's largest oil spills. They are less frequent than other kinds of oil spills, such as pipeline breaks, but typically involve large volumes of spilled oil relative to other kinds of oil spills.

The amount of oil from different types of spills can vary from year to year.

Between 1971 and 2000, tankers and barges were responsible for 45 percent of the volume of oil spilled in U.S. waters, according to a 2002 U.S. Department of the Interior Minerals Management Service report.

In that same period, pipelines were responsible for 16 percent of the volume of oil spilled in U.S. waters. This includes both onshore and offshore pipelines, though onshore spills accounted for most of the pipeline spillage into U.S. waters—92 percent or more in each decade.

Between 1971 and 2000, U.S. Outer Continental Shelf (OCS) offshore facilities and pipelines accounted for only 2 percent of the volume of oil spilled in U.S. waters.

The amount of oil from different types of spills can vary from year to year.

Where do most oil spills happen in the world?

Analysts for the Oil Spill Intelligence Report have reported that spills in that size range have occurred in the waters of

112 nations since 1960. But certain areas see more spills than others. The Report identifies these "hot spots" for oil spills from vessels:

- Gulf of Mexico (267 spills)

- Northeastern U.S. (140 spills)

- Mediterranean Sea (127 spills)

- Persian Gulf (108 spills)

- North Sea (75 spills)

- Japan (60 spills)

- Baltic Sea (52 spills)

- United Kingdom and English Channel (49 spills)

- Malaysia and Singapore (39 spills)

- West coast of France and north and west coasts of Spain (33 spills)

- Korea (32 spills)

Early American Spills

When was the first oil spill in the United States?

While no one is certain of the answer, oil experts have suggested some possibilities, including natural oil seeps that were in the water even before man-made ones, according to NOAA.

In the early 1500s, the Portuguese-born explorer Juan Cabrillo sailed into what is now Santa Barbara, California, and remarked on the oil he saw bubbling out from a natural seep.

In 1859, the first U.S. oil well was drilled near Titusville, Pennsylvania. And it's possible the first oil spills occurred while the crude oil was transported from this well.

Around 1889 or 1890, the steamer Albatross reported a massive oil slick extending from L.A. south to northern San Diego County though the source of the slick is unknown.

On Dec. 13, 1907, the Thomas W. Lawson, a seven-masted steel schooner bound for London and loaded with oil was caught in a storm and stranded on the Scilly Islands, England.

In 1929, a 600-barrel oil spill covered 9 miles (14 km) off Ventura County Beach in California. By 1930, spills from ships were considered a greater menace than shoreline leakage, according to NOAA.

Where does oil come from originally?

Scientists aren't sure. Contrary to popular explanations, it's not mostly from dinosaurs. Oil is thought to be the result of chemical processes affecting remnants of tiny organisms—such as plankton in the sea—that lived millions of years ago. But scientists admit they're not sure how oil was made.

The Gulf Oil Spill Illustrates the Special Risks of Deepwater Drilling

Charles H. Peterson et al.

Charles H. Peterson is alumni distinguished professor of marine sciences, biology, and ecology at the University of North Carolina at Chapel Hill. He has published nearly two hundred papers in peer-reviewed journals and books and has served on several governmental commissions and study panels of the US National Academy of Sciences.

The *Deepwater Horizon* (DWH) well blowout in the Gulf of Mexico represents a tale of two spills: the traditional shore-bound surface spill and the novel deep-ocean persistence of intrusions of finely dispersed (atomized) oil, gas, and dispersants. The discharge of oil and gas under high pressure at 1500-meter (m) water depth makes the DWH incident categorically different from all previous well-studied crude oil releases into the sea. Implementation of legislatively mandated natural resource damage assessment revealed serious gaps in the baseline information on deep-sea communities, their functioning, and their ecotoxicological vulnerability, which demonstrates a need to modify the laws and policies intended to sustain ecosystem services that are at risk from oil and gas drilling.

Before the DWH incident, the prevailing scientific model of maritime oil behavior, fate, and exposure pathways and the consequent impacts on natural resources reflected a synthetic understanding of historical oil spills as occurring typically on the surface or in shallow, nearshore waters. In traditional spills, crude oil rises rapidly to or remains at the sea surface, and gaseous hydrocarbons escape into the atmosphere with minimal residence time in the water column. Organisms that occupy or frequently encounter the sea surface, such as floating seabirds, can suffer high mortality rates. On landfall, this generally cohesive surface oil fouls intertidal and shallow subtidal habitats, which degrades ecosystem services by killing sensitive organisms, including key providers of structural habitat, such as salt-marsh macrophytes and mangroves. Oil can persist when it is buried in anoxic, nutrient-limited sediments, where weathering is inhibited, leading to chronic biological exposures that can reduce production or reproductive output and indirectly suppress the population recovery of exposed animals for decades by depressing their fitness.

> *The [Deepwater Horizon] disaster breaks the prevailing mold of traditional shallow-water spills.*

Depth Makes a Difference

In stark contrast, the DWH blowout occurred in deep (1500 m) offshore waters, where a highly turbulent discharge of hot, pressurized oil and gas entrained cold seawater under high pressures and produced a variety of dispersed phases, including small oil droplets, gas bubbles, oil-gas emulsions, and gas hydrates. An injection of 0.77 million gallons of chemical dispersants at the wellhead, beginning 24 days after the well blowout, also contributed to the dispersion of the oil. The collective buoyancy of the oil and gas created a rising plume, but unlike a continuous-phase (e.g., sewage) plume, much of the oil and gas separated from the entrained seawater as it apparently became trapped by depth-related physical discontinuities and was deflected laterally by ambient currents. The dissolution into seawater of water-soluble petroleum compounds, including most of the methane, ethane, and propane and large fractions of water-soluble aromatic compounds, explains the elevated levels of petroleum hydrocarbons retained in the sub-surface plume at a water depth of 1100 m. A plume of hydrocarbon-enriched waters was observed by others at depths of 800–1200 m, at which hydrocarbons stimulated intense heterotrophic microbial activity and may have entered deep-sea food chains through pelagic primary consumers. The occurrence of a deepwater spill of this magnitude and with these characteristics is unprecedented and clearly warrants a new conceptual oil spill model. Although about half of the 4.9 million barrels of DWH oil did rise to the sea surface, it became weathered during ascent, such that the oil reaching the surface appeared reddish-brown in color and was less cohesive than crude oil discharged onto the surface would be. Liquid oil droplets enriched with denser compounds, such as asphaltenes, descended toward the seafloor. In addition, the process of the agglomeration of oil particles, sediments, drilling muds, and marine snow (detritus falling through the water column), mediated by adhesive bacterial exudates, also triggered oil transport to the seafloor, where deposition of polycyclic aromatic hydrocarbon-enriched particulates appears to be associated with the death of hard- and soft-bottom invertebrates.

A Sense of Urgency

Although the DWH disaster breaks the prevailing mold of traditional shallow-water spills, the international petroleum industry has already transferred the focus of its marine exploration and production activities to deep (i.e., greater than 305 m) and ultradeep (i.e., greater than 500 m) fields, especially in the Gulf of Mexico, as nearshore shallow-water reservoirs have become depleted. This redirection of ocean drilling in the oil and gas industry underscores the urgency to elaborate further details of the new oil spill model as a policy priority to prepare for future risk assessments and well blowouts. Evaluating how massive the impacts of organic carbon loading, the taxon-dependent toxicity of multiple hydrocarbons and dispersants, and physical fouling are on a poorly understood pelagic and benthic deepwater ecosystem requires an enhanced scientific understanding.

A failure to take advantage of the DWH disaster as a massive, unplanned, and otherwise indefensible experiment would represent a missed opportunity to understand ecological and societal implications of this and future deepwater blowouts.

The unexpected aspects and unknowns associated with deepwater ecosystems and the high-pressure petroleum releases during the DWH well blowout posed unanticipated challenges to the governmental response, which was dictated by federal legislation based on experience arising from traditional oil spills. In the United States, the Oil Pollution Act (OPA) of 1990 articulates policies that specify collaboration among federal, state, and tribal governments, together with the parties responsible for the oil spill, to assess impacts and achieve restoration. A sequence of actions implements those policies in the process known as NRDA. NRDA is intended to achieve the following: (a) a minimization of environmental injury through emergency responses; (b) the use of defensible science to quantify damages to natural resources and their ecosystem and human services; (c) the provision through negotiation or litigation of a financial settlement sufficient to achieve compensatory restoration; and then (d) the implementation of restoration projects designed to replace losses of natural resources and of ecosystem services. The report of the presidential National Commission on the BP *Deepwater Horizon* Oil Spill and Offshore Drilling documented many policy failings of the Minerals Management Service (MMS; now split into two independent agencies: the Bureau of Ocean Energy Management, and the Bureau of Safety and Environmental Enforcement), including, for example, the agency's failure to require in advance of deepwater drilling approval that drillers demonstrate the availability of tested technologies to terminate a deepwater blowout. Here, we document how and why the NRDA process is challenged by a well blowout in the deep sea and, by extension, other unfamiliar pollution events at environmental frontiers. . . .

Gaps in Knowledge

Several serious gaps in scientific understanding exist that inhibited the capacity of the NRDA process to determine the ecosystem impacts of the DWH well blowout and that may have prevented the collection of the information necessary to detail all the important damages to the deepwater pelagic and benthic resources and their ecosystem functions. First, detailed understanding of the physicochemical behavior of oil, gas, and dispersants when they are released under the environmental conditions that prevailed at the wellhead is incomplete. Second, knowledge of the transport and fate of oil and gas depends on the challenging task of coupling dynamic changes in buoyancy with accurate, real-time, three-dimensional physical circulation models of the ocean. Third, quantitative measures of the dispersion of oil into fine droplets and the creation of subsurface oil-gas-water-gas-hydrate emulsions that, to some degree, resulted in seafloor deposition are needed in order to depict the fate of the released hydrocarbons and the extent of biological exposures. . . .

A Call for More Research

Much more research is needed to provide the scientific capacity to assess impacts of deepwater blowouts. Pursuing such research will prove costly, complex, and demanding of limited research platforms and technology. Assessing impacts acting through food web modifications, persistence of toxicants, and biogeochemical transformations may require relatively long time frames as lagged indirect effects play out over multiple years. Multiyear investments in research do not fit comfortably within the traditional NRDA practices under the OPA, which contemplates familiar, more-accessible ecosystems of shallow waters and shorelines, where traditional approaches may suffice. A failure to take advantage of the DWH disaster as a massive, unplanned, and otherwise indefensible experiment would represent a missed opportunity to understand ecological and societal implications of this and future deepwater blowouts.

Tar Sands Oil Makes Pipelines More Vulnerable to Spills

Keith Schneider

Keith Schneider is a former national correspondent and regular contributor to The New York Times. *He is senior editor of Circle of Blue, an independent, nonpartisan journalism organization that focuses primarily on water-related issues. He also writes a popular blog, called* ModeShift *(www.modeshift.org), about energy, transportation, climate, and environmental policy.*

Just after dawn on July 26, 2010, homeowners along Talmadge Creek near Marshall, Michigan, awoke to the chemical stench of raw fuel. Several bolted outside and followed the sickening stink to the creek's wooded banks and found its source: a torrent of black goo, unlike anything ever experienced in Michigan or anywhere else in the upper Midwest, heading downstream to the Kalamazoo River.

The black goo originated some 2,000 miles away, in the tar sands fields of Alberta, Canada. There, a massive extraction effort has damaged thousands of square miles of forests, polluted water supplies, and poured tens of thousands of tons of greenhouse gas emissions into the atmosphere each year—all in an effort to provide a new source of transportation fuel to quench American demands, as well as alleviate concerns about reliance on oil from the Middle East and find energy sources closer to home.

Water Supplies Put at Risk

What the Michigan spill revealed, however, is that an expanding constellation of processing plants, refineries, and transcontinental pipelines needed to produce and transport tar sands oil to American markets also puts communities and water supplies across the U.S. at risk. And it's a risk that, until recently, was little known or understood by the communities that stand in harm's way.

In a new report released today [February 16, 2011], NRDC [Natural Resources Defense Council] and several partner groups demonstrate that tar sands oil is more difficult and dangerous to transport than conventional crude. Known as DilBit, short for diluted bitumen, it's thick as peanut butter and more acidic, highly corrosive, and abrasive. Yet the NRDC report says that pipeline developers and operators are using the same designs, operating practices, and materials to transport DilBit that work for conventional crude.

Tar sands oil requires extensive processing before it can be used as transportation fuel.

Those practices might have contributed to the deterioration of the steel pipeline outside of Marshall and its rupture last summer—a disaster that's now considered the worst oil spill in Midwest history and caused more than $500 million in damage. If changes aren't made, the result could be more accidents, spills, and polluted waterways, says the report, which calls for a moratorium on pipeline development until stronger safety measures and regulations can be developed.

"Because people in the United States hadn't had any experience with raw tar sands oil, they didn't know how dangerous it can be," said Anthony Swift, an NRDC tar sands expert and co-author of the study, prepared with the help of two other national environmental organizations and the Pipeline Safety Trust, a nonprofit group that works with the pipeline industry to increase safety.

Huge Tar Sands Reserve

The Alberta tar sands conservatively contain 175 billion barrels of recoverable oil. That's enough to satisfy U.S. demand at

current rates of consumption—7 billion barrels annually—
until 2035. Energy companies say they intend to more than
double production from 1.5 million barrels a day currently to
more than 3 million barrels per day by 2025. But tar sands oil
requires extensive processing before it can be used as transportation fuel, and Canadian refineries have reached capacity,
so U.S. and European oil companies are spending $20 billion
to expand and retrofit refineries in the Midwest and Texas
Gulf to turn tar sands into oil.

But first, they have to get it there, which requires a costly
and expansive pipeline network. During the past year, Enbridge, a Canadian pipeline developer that owns the pipe that
ruptured in Michigan, opened a $1.2 billion, 1,000-mile pipe-
line from Alberta to Superior, Wisconsin. Enbridge's main
competitor, TransCanada, opened a $5 billion, 2,147-mile
pipeline known as Keystone to refineries in Illinois and storage depots in Oklahoma. The company wants to build a third
major pipeline, known as Keystone XL, nearly 2,000 miles
from Alberta to Oklahoma and onward to the Gulf Coast, at a
cost of $7 billion.

---

*Communities from Montana to Texas in the path of
pipeline development are beginning to raise questions
about safety.*

Transporting DilBit

Oil companies are now shipping 500,000 barrels of DilBit
daily to U.S. refineries. The peanut butter-thick substance contains 15 to 20 times higher acid concentrations than conventional crude oil, five to 10 times as much sulfur, high concentrations of chloride salts, and higher concentrations of abrasive
quartz sand particles.

"This combination of chemical corrosion and physical abrasion can dramatically increase the rate of pipeline deterioration," the NRDC report says.

In order to get it to flow through pipelines, raw tar sands bitumen is diluted with natural gas condensate and then moved in heated pipelines under high pressure. The study asserts that the higher temperatures and higher internal pipeline pressures can create gas bubbles within the pipelines, deform the metal, and lead to ruptures caused by pressure spikes.

The report's authors found convincing statistical evidence of the hazards of transporting DilBit. From 2002 to 2008, Alberta's pipeline system, which has a longer record of transporting the raw diluted bitumen, experienced 218 spills per 10,000 miles of pipeline. That was a rate of spills from corrosion approximately 16 times greater than the 13.8 corrosion-related spills during the same period along the same length of pipeline in the U.S.

Oil Industry Is Silent on Report's Findings

Canadian pipeline builders, the U.S. Department of Transportation, and the American Petroleum Institute did not respond to repeated email and telephone messages seeking comments about the report's findings.

But communities from Montana to Texas in the path of pipeline development are beginning to raise questions about safety. Several member of Congress, too, have expressed concern. New Jersey Democratic Senator Frank R. Lautenberg introduced a bill [in February 2011]—Pipeline Transportation Safety Improvement Act of 2011—that would require a full assessment of whether federal safeguards are adequate for tar sands crude.

This new activism comes as the State Department considers TransCanada's proposal to build Keystone XL, the first big tar sands pipeline to attract intense public scrutiny. The two earlier tar sands pipelines were quickly granted permits to cross the U.S. border with Canada during the [George] Bush administration.

Keystone Pipeline Faces Scrutiny

On July 16, 2010—just 10 days before the Kalamazoo spill—the U.S. Environmental Protection Agency issued an 18-page letter that directed the State Department to more carefully assess the considerable risks to wetlands, rivers, and communities. The proposed pipeline route crosses native prairie in Kansas and South Dakota, endangered whooping crane habitat along the Platte River in Nebraska, and runs past dozens of small towns.

The State Department is expected early this year to decide how to proceed with its environmental and safety review for Keystone XL. Susan Casey-Lefkowitz, director of NRDC's International Program, who has studied tar sands issues extensively and is a recognized national expert, said she expects the State Department to undertake additional studies and open a public comment period that could last up to 90 days.

In Michigan, meanwhile, people are still contending with the consequences of last summer's spill. Residents have filed more than 2,370 claims on everything from medical bills to hotel stays to property repairs as a result of the accident, according to company figures. A class-action lawsuit is in development. Enbridge said its cleanup costs could reach $550 million, according to Canadian press reports. All but $35 million to $45 million will be paid by its insurers. Cleanup work is continuing and, the company has bought out 71 homeowners whose property was affected.

The company repaired the rupture and reopened the pipeline in September [2010]. The Suncor refinery in Sarnia, Canada, and the BP refinery in Whiting, Indiana, have resumed processing DilBit into fuel.

The Biggest Oil Spill in History Was Deliberately Caused

Counterspill

Founded by documentary filmmaker Chris Paine, Counterspill is an online project that focuses on documenting the impact of nonrenewable energy disasters. The organization's goal is to create a "counter-narrative that takes on corporate and governmental spin."

At the end of January 1991, reports of a huge oil spill in the Persian Gulf began to surface. Iraqi forces purposefully opened valves at the Sea Island oil terminal and dumped oil from several tankers into the Persian Gulf in a strategic wartime move against U.S. forces.

The U.S. accused the Iraqis of committing "environmental terrorism" by intentionally spilling several million barrels of oil. Administration sources also commented that an incendiary strike could be carried out against the spill, in an effort to burn oil before it reached key industrial facilities, including water purification plants, in the area. Iraqi officials blamed the U.S. for starting the spill via a recent bombing, however American officials denied the claim, as spilling oil didn't "do anything militarily."

In a disaster already nearly inaccessible due to the war zone surrounding it, February's (1991) cleanup efforts to slow the effect of the spill were further hampered by poor coordination and lack of accessible funds. Alleged bureaucratic friction is said to have further exasperated efforts, however Saudi officials were quick to maintain that the situation was under control, reports *The New York Times.*

Southerly winds kept the 60-mile-long slick in place, but environmentalists were concerned that no preventative measures took place.

The Coast Guard commented that people who had seen the oil were "amazed" at the amount.

"Only the Environment Suffers"

On March 2, [1991] Dr. Abdulbar Al Gain of the Saudi Arabian Meteorology and Environmental Protection Administration assured the public that the Arabian Gulf "has not been destroyed environmentally" but they conceded that it would probably take years for the environment to return to its natural state. Estimated spillage remained speculative, and reports decreased the amount of oil to 3 million barrels. Al Gain confirmed that the oil unleashed served no military purpose, as "only the environment suffers."

Although the area surrounding Gulf War Oil Spill was finally cleared of strife relating to the war, the cleanup response remained slow-going. At an environmental conference between U.S. and Saudi officials on March 7, some commented that the amount of labor required to handle a disaster of its size was not available in the region, due to reconstruction efforts related to the war.

The Coast Guard commented that people who had seen the oil were "amazed" at the amount, however estimates still remained wildly speculative.

Burning Wells in Kuwait

Meanwhile, the Kuwaiti Oil Fires blazed. Red Adair, legendary oil well firefighter, complained about the lack of a reliable chain of command while fighting the fires.

The firefighting team started in the northeastern region of wells and planned to move toward the larger, more unwieldy fires of the southwest. At that point, 175 of an estimated 500 fiery wells were controlled, however Adair said the process would be more effective if the Kuwaiti Oil Co. did not put bids out for equipment needed.

The oceanic oil slick inched toward containment. Confident that most of the oil that had accumulated in the water was dissipated, Saudi Arabia began to put away serpentine booms that had been used as shields from contamination. Some booms would still remain around water filtering and desalination plants. Although the amount spilled was still unknown at that point, at least 2 million barrels of "weathered" oil had been accumulated. Twenty-one skimming boats had also been deployed to the region, in order to search for oil patches.

Paul Horsman, a Greenpeace activist, surveyed 240 miles of Persian Gulf shoreline before telling the *Chicago Sun-Times* that some parts were "beyond repair."

Saudi officials announced that beach cleanup response would start in September [1991], saying that over 1.7 million barrels had already been removed from the sea. Horsman was doubtful that the cleanup would make a difference as he said most areas were beyond recovery due to the delay.

Closing Ceremonies

All oil wells damaged due to the Gulf War were officially shut down on November 7 [1991]. Burgan 118, an oil well specifically reignited for the event, was ceremoniously shut down by Sheik Jaber al-Ahmed al-Sabah, the emir of Kuwait. The oil minister proclaimed that the natural resources of the area were officially protected and a full ecological survey was still being carried out. The ceremony included musical accompaniments of bagpipes and tambourines, and the emir walked down a red carpet to shut down the well.

The cost of dousing the Kuwaiti oil fires amounted to more than $1.5 billion. More than 700 wells were capped, and firefighters used over a billion gallons of water to put out the oil fires.

As of March 2011, [the] cleanup is far from over.

Even so, over 200 lakes of oil formed throughout the desert due to the massive amounts of spillage, some more than 6 feet deep. By the end of 1991, the massive cloud of smoke that had formed during the fires was starting to dissipate, but many in the local population continued to complain of respiratory problems.

As of March 2011, cleanup is far from over. According to Arab News, the Saudi government set contracts worth 700 million Saudi Riyal (over $180 million) to rehabilitate the environments decimated by the Gulf War. The UN contributed $45 million.

By the Numbers

Resources lost PER DAY from the Kuwaiti Oil Fires could have . . .

- FUELED A CAR FOR 214,500 YEARS, [WHICH EQUALS] 7,312,500 TANKS, [WHICH EQUALS] 117,000,000 GALLONS OF GAS

- FUELED A JET FOR 7,200,000 MILES, [WHICH EQUALS] 193 TRIPS AROUND THE GLOBE, [WHICH EQUALS] 24,000,000 GALLONS OF JET FUEL

- BOUGHT 57 WIND TURBINES, [WHICH COULD POWER] 20,833 HOMES FOR A YEAR [or] AN ELECTRIC CAR FOR 78.2 MILLION MILES, [WHICH EQUALS] $115,000,000

CHAPTER 2

Is the Risk of a Spill Worth Drilling for Oil?

Americans Split on Energy vs. Environment Trade-Off

Jeffrey M. Jones

Jeffrey M. Jones is an analyst for the Gallup opinion poll organization.

Americans are about as likely to say production of energy supplies (47%) should be prioritized as to say environmental protection (44%) should be, a closer division than last year, when energy led by 50% to 41%. These views mark a shift compared with the early 2000s, when Americans consistently assigned a higher priority to environmental protection.

The greater preference for energy production over environmental protection in recent years likely results from the economic downturn, given that Americans have made economic matters their highest priority. There was a brief exception in the spring of 2010, however, after the Gulf of Mexico oil spill brought environmental issues back to the forefront.

Although Americans still view the economy as their No. 1 concern, they percieve the economy to be improving. In this context, the public is now about evenly divided on whether energy development or the environment should be given priority.

These results are based on Gallup's annual Environment poll, conducted March 8–11 [2012]. Rising gas prices, debate over government approval of the Keystone XL pipeline, and President Obama's current energy policy tour highlight the importance of the energy issue. The Keystone issue in particular has reminded Americans about the trade-offs between increased energy production and risks to the environment.

Democrats and Republicans take opposing sides on the issue, with Republicans favoring energy development by 68% to 24% and Democrats preferring environmental protection by 56% to 34%. Independents' views are closer to those of Democrats, with 49% prioritizing the environment and 41% energy production.

Compared with 10 years ago, when Americans overall favored environmental protection by 12 percentage points (52% to 40%), all groups have moved in the direction of energy prioritization, though Republicans have shifted much more so than either independents or Democrats.

Americans continue to say the U.S. should emphasize energy conservation by consumers over increased production of oil, gas, and coal to address the nation's energy problems.

Public Assigns Higher Priority to Alternative Energy, Conservation Than Production

Americans favor more environmentally friendly energy solutions when they are presented with various choices for addressing the nation's energy problems.

First, Americans are nearly twice as likely to say the United States should put greater emphasis on the development of alternative energy supplies such as wind and solar power (59%) as to say the U.S. should emphasize production of more oil, gas, and coal supplies (34%). This is the case even though Republicans are more likely to favor production of traditional energy sources over alternative energy.

Gallup found a 66% to 26% margin in favor of alternative energy among all Americans last year, the first time the question was asked.

Also, Americans continue to say the U.S. should emphasize energy conservation by consumers over increased production of oil, gas, and coal to address the nation's energy problems. However, the 11-point gap in favor of conservation this year (51% to 40%) is much smaller than it was from 2001–2008, when it averaged just under 30 points.

The reduced gap in favor of conservation is due mostly to Republicans' changing preferences. Republicans currently prefer energy production by 63% to 29%. In 2002, Republicans said conservation should be emphasized over production, by 53% to 35%.

Independents have shifted slightly away from conservation, while Democrats' preferences are essentially the same as they were 10 years ago.

Americans as a whole show a proclivity for more environmentally friendly approaches to dealing with the energy situation.

Implications

Americans now split about evenly when asked to choose between an emphasis on increased energy production and environmental protection. These preferences have varied in the past 11 years in response to changes in the health of the economy and to dramatic events such as the Gulf of Mexico oil spill.

Politics have also played a part in Americans' shifting preferences over the past decade, with Republicans increasingly coming down on the side of increased production of oil, gas, and coal. This likely reflects party leaders' preference for increased oil exploration in U.S. coastal areas and on U.S. land, which was a key focus at the 2008 Republican National Convention and more recently in calls by Republican presidential candidates and congressional leaders for the government to approve the Keystone XL pipeline.

But Americans as a whole show a proclivity for more environmentally friendly approaches to dealing with the energy situation, including a greater focus on energy conservation or developing alternative energy supplies, even though Republicans take the opposing view.

Survey Methods

Results for this Gallup poll are based on telephone interviews conducted March 8–11, 2012, with a random sample of 1,024 adults, aged 18 and older, living in all 50 U.S. states and the District of Columbia.

For results based on the total sample of national adults, one can say with 95% confidence that the maximum margin of sampling error is ±4 percentage points.

Interviews are conducted with respondents on landline telephones and cellular phones, with interviews conducted in Spanish for respondents who are primarily Spanish-speaking. Each sample includes a minimum quota of 400 cell phone respondents and 600 landline respondents per 1,000 national adults, with additional minimum quotas among landline respondents by region. Landline telephone numbers are chosen at random among listed telephone numbers. Cell phone numbers are selected using random-digit-dial methods. Landline respondents are chosen at random within each household on the basis of which member had the most recent birthday.

Samples are weighted by gender, age, race, Hispanic ethnicity, education, region, adults in the household, and phone status (cell phone only/landline only/ both, cell phone mostly, and having an unlisted landline number). Demographic weighting targets are based on the March 2011 Current Population Survey figures for the aged 18 and older non-institutionalized population living in U.S. telephone households. All reported margins of sampling error include the computed design effects for weighting and sample design.

In addition to sampling error, question wording and practical difficulties in conducting surveys can introduce error or bias into the findings of public opinion polls.

Offshore Drilling Remains a Risk Worth Taking

Ronald Bailey

Ronald Bailey is a science correspondent for Reason *magazine and the author of the book* Liberation Biology: The Scientific and Moral Case for the Biotech Revolution.

Two weeks ago [April 20, 2010] BP's Deepwater Horizon oil drilling rig in the Gulf of Mexico exploded, killing 11 workers. The exploratory well began gushing oil at an estimated rate of 5,000 barrels per day when the blowout prevention system failed. The growing oil slick menaces the marshes and beaches of Louisiana, Mississippi, Alabama and Florida. Should the slick come ashore, previous research suggests the deleterious effects on fisheries and wildlife would be substantial and long-lasting.

As someone who has enjoyed the sugar white sands of Alabama's beaches, it is a terrible shame that they are at risk of being despoiled by oily muck. But as someone who also enjoys the conveniences of modern civilization including the on-demand mobility offered by airplanes and automobiles that enable me to visit those beaches, I understand trade-offs.

Knee-jerk Reactions

Opponents of offshore drilling have jumped on the spill as evidence that offshore drilling is inherently dangerous, and not worth the risk. They see the blowout as evidence that the recently lifted moratorium on offshore drilling in parts of the outer continental shelf should be reinstated. Miyoko Sakashita of the Center for Biological Diversity decried "the absurdity of the claims by the oil industry and politicians beholden to that industry that offshore oil and gas development is safe." As a consequence, the center is urging the [Barack] Obama administration "to reinstitute a moratorium on new offshore oil leasing, exploration, and development on all our coasts." The Natural Resources Defense Council is also calling for a "time-out" on any further offshore oil drilling until an independent investigation of the BP spill is completed. On April 30, the Obama administration heeded the call for a time-out and halted plans to expand offshore drilling until an investigation into the causes of the BP blowout are complete.

But in deciding whether or not to continue offshore exploration for oil and gas, a calm quantitative approach makes more sense than a rush to ban drilling after seeing some pictures of oily birds. It would be useful to figure out if the costs, economic and ecological, outweigh the benefits of producing offshore oil and gas. Luckily, a recent study by Georgetown University economist Robert Hahn and Milken Institute economist Peter Passell offers some insight to this question. Published in the December 2009 issue of *Energy Economics,* their study "The economics of allowing more U.S. oil drilling," finds that the benefits of producing offshore oil greatly outweigh the costs.

At $50 per barrel the benefits of producing 10 billion barrels of offshore oil would be $323 billion greater than its costs.

The Economics of Oil Production

In their analysis, Hahn and Passell look at three types of benefits: producer revenues, lower prices to consumers, and less fluctuation in oil prices. These benefits are considered in a scenario in which oil is priced at $50 per barrel, and in another in which it goes for $100 per barrel. (The current price is around $85 per barrel.) At $50 per barrel they estimate that 10 billion barrels of oil would be recoverable from the off-limits outer continental shelf, and at $100 this rises to 11.5 billion barrels.

On the cost side of the ledger they calculate that it would cost $17 per barrel to produce offshore oil at $50 per barrel and $20 per barrel at $100 per barrel. They incorporate a Minerals Management Service estimate of $700 million as the cost of the environmental damage caused by producing 10 billion barrels of oil offshore. They include an estimate of damage caused by greenhouse gases produced by burning the oil as fuel, and the direct costs of local air pollution, and traffic congestion and accidents. So what did they find?

A Cost-Benefit Analysis

At $50 per barrel, the benefits of offshore oil production in the formerly off limits areas of the outer continental shelf would garner $492 billion in revenues, $42 billion in lower oil prices, and reduce the cost of oil price disruptions by $42 billion, yielding total benefits of $578 billion. The direct drilling costs would come to $166 billion, environmental costs $1 billion, greenhouse gas damages $1 billion, local air pollution $28 billion, traffic congestion $28 billion, and traffic accidents $32 billion, for a total cost amounting to $255 billion. So at $50 per barrel the benefits of producing 10 billion barrels of offshore oil would be $323 billion greater than its costs.

At $100 per barrel, outer continental shelf oil production of 11.5 billion barrels of oil would reap $1.15 trillion in revenues, lower oil prices by $99 billion, and reduce the costs price disruptions by $51 billion, resulting in total benefits of $1.3 trillion. Drilling costs would be $238 billion, environmental costs and greenhouse gas damages would total $2 billion, the costs of local air pollution, traffic congestion, and traffic accidents would be $22 billion, $33 billion, and $38 billion respectively. So the total costs of producing 11.5 billion barrels of offshore oil would be $332 billion. Hahn and Passell calculate that at $100 per barrel, the net benefits of producing offshore oil would come to $967 billion, or a trillion dollars. They note that even if the total costs were doubled in both scenarios, "the qualitative conclusion that resource development passes any plausible benefit-cost test still holds."

But perhaps the environmental costs used by Hahn and Passell are too low. Could they be wrong about the cost of greenhouse emissions? Hahn and Passell note that even at the highest social cost of carbon at $321 per ton suggested by British economist Nicholas Stern, the total benefits of producing offshore oil are still positive. In that case, the net benefits drop from $325 billion to $120 billion at $50 per barrel, and from $975 billion to $725 billion at $100 per barrel.

Increasing safety results from learning how to make better trade-offs over time between risks.

As for other environmental impacts, analysts at the Environmental Protection Agency (EPA) have devised a Basic Oil Spill Cost Estimation Model to try to figure out the costs of various types of spills. For example, the EPA model projects that the socioeconomic costs of spills over a million gallons is about $60 per gallon and the environmental costs are $30 per gallon. So if the BP blowout continues as-is for a total of 50 days, it will spew 10 million gallons into the Gulf, resulting in $900 million in costs. Applying the model's highest socioeconomic sensitivity adjustment factor of 2 raises those costs to $1.2 billion, and applying the EPA formula including the highest vulnerability (wildlife) and habitat sensitivity factor (wetlands) raises those costs to nearly $1 billion, for a total of $2.2 billion.

The Price of Exxon Valdez

This figure is basically the same as the total clean up costs of the biggest oil spill in U.S. history: In 1989, the Exxon Valdez oil tanker leaked 250,000 barrels of crude oil (about 10 million gallons) after being run aground on a reef in Alaska's Prince William Sound. The BP blowout will eclipse the Exxon Valdez spill if it continues flowing for another 33 days. The ultimate clean up costs for the Exxon Valdez accident amounted to about $2.2 billion, with additional legal costs and damage payments of $2.3 billion. Some analysts are estimating that the costs for clean up and payment for economic losses from the BP spill might reach as high as $12.5 billion. As it should be, BP's corporate leadership has declared that the company will be responsible for paying for the costs of the spill. [By January 2013, actual costs for cleanup, fines, and economic loss were approaching $30 billion.]

In his book, *Normal Accidents: Living with High Risk Technologies* (1984), Yale University sociologist Charles Perrow noted that when a technology fails, it often does so because "the problem is just something that never occurred to the designers." Assuming no malfeasance, whatever went wrong with the Deepwater Horizon drill rig will likely uncover just such a problem and future designers will fix it. Progress is a trial and error process, and increasing safety results from learning how to make better trade-offs over time between risks. Despite this current disaster, offshore oil drilling remains a risk well worth taking.

Despite Spills, More Oil Sands Pipelines Are Coming

Christopher Helman

Christopher Helman has been a staff writer for Forbes *magazine since 1999, primarily covering the energy industry and the major players who control it.*

Last week [June 2012] Canadian pipeline giant Enbridge suffered a leak on its Athabasca pipeline that carries 350,000 barrels of crude from the Alberta oil sands region over the border into the United States. Roughly 1,400 barrels of oil escaped the line in a rural area. The oil is being cleaned up. Harder to clean up: the reputational damage to a company that tries to depict pipelines as a safe and effective way to get Canada's oil sands crude to market.

Enbridge is not the company behind the controversial Keystone XL pipeline. That project belongs to TransCanada. Four years ago Enbridge had its own oil sands lines into the United States approved without any such hoopla. "It was a non-issue," says Leon Zupan, president of Enbridge's gas pipeline business and former senior v.p. of its oil pipelines.

Enbridge, among its $34 billion in assets, owns the Athabasca and Wapasu lines, which together import 700,000 barrels per day of oil sands crude into the U.S. "We are the largest developer and operator of pipelines out of the oil sands," Zupan told me in an interview a few days before the recent leak.

What's more, Enbridge moves a total of 1.2 million bpd to the U.S. from Canada. "If Enbridge was a country we would be the largest importer to the U.S.," says Zupan. "13% of total U.S. imports come through the Enbridge system, more than from Saudi Arabia."

Extensive Pipeline System

Adding in conventional Canadian crude and oil from the Bakken formation of North Dakota and Montana and Enbridge's U.S. pipeline system handles more than 2 million bpd and covers thousands of miles.

Within five years Enbridge hopes to be bringing 2 million bpd of oil sands crude into the US to feed refineries.

Unfortunately no giant system can be 100% leak-proof. In addition to last week's 1,400 barrel spill, in 2010 an Enbridge line leaked 20,000 barrels into Michigan's Kalamazoo River. The river cleanup cost roughly $700 million so far. (In contrast recall that BP's Macondo blowout was leaking 50,000 bpd into the Gulf of Mexico, for a total of roughly 2 million barrels.)

The new spill doesn't help the p.r. campaign that Enbridge is waging in Canada to seek approvals for its Northern Gateway line that would carry oil sands crude 650 miles from Alberta to the Pacific coast port of Kitimat—crossing pristine wilderness and lands traditionally held by First Nations tribes.

As part of $3 billion in expansion projects, Enbridge also plans to expand the line that leaked into the Kalamazoo as well as "twin" its existing Athabasca and Wapasu lines, doubling their capacity. Within five years Enbridge hopes to be bringing 2 million bpd of oil sands crude into the U.S. to feed refineries like BP's Whiting, Indiana plant that have undergone costly overhauls to be able to break down the heavy crude.

And Enbridge won't be the only one. Zupan thinks the northern stretch of the Keystone XL line will get built. It is to carry another 800,000 bpd from the oil sands to the U.S.

Differing Visions of Progress

Environmentalists, naturally, oppose any development of the oil sands, which contain more heavy metals and contaminants than conventional crude oil. "Tar sands oil corrodes pipelines, creating a greater risk of devastating oil spills along the route," said Danielle Droitsch, senior attorney with the Natural Resources Defense Council in a statement last week. "We cannot afford to ignore the climate and environmental dangers that come with the increasing amounts of tar sands oil being pushed into the United States."

For all the hate that environmentalists direct toward the oil sands, the pipeline companies love them. The resource is enormous enough to support production of 4 million bpd for 150 years. They know that the pipelines they lay now will wear out and have to be replaced long before the oil sands are depleted. And because of the nature of oil sands development they know that once an oil sands project is built and starts producing, it's not going to be shut down.

"It doesn't have an on or off switch based on the price of gas or oil today. You may be chasing cash flow, but it's going to flow," says Terrance McGill, president of U.S. subsidiary Enbridge Energy Company.

Oil Sands Extraction Is Expensive

The reason for this is simple: the upfront costs of oil sands are enormous, more per barrel than any other oil development, so once those development costs are sunk in the ground and the infrastructure is built, the oil companies will work it at full capacity in order to make back their investment.

Witness ExxonMobil's giant Kearl development. Exxon expects to finish the first 100,000 bpd phase of Kearl later this year at a cost of roughly $10 billion. In time, and after two more expansions, Kearl will produce 350,000 bpd, and with more than 5 billion barrels of recoverable resources, will be able to keep it up for 40 years.

The U.S. would be stupid not to take full advantage of this reliable oil supply to the north.

Because of this massive upfront investment, oil sands are very different from America's crop of shale plays like the Bakken, Marcellus and Eagle Ford. A good well in the Bakken might start off flowing 3,000 bpd, but rates fall off more than 50% in the first year. To keep production up, drillers have to keep drilling, and that decision to drill or not to drill is informed by today's oil and gas prices.

There's no such quandry with oil sands. The pipeline companies know it will be produced, and the refiners know it will be there for them to refine. Refiners in the Midwest have upgraded to take oil sands crude, while those down on the Gulf Coast and California see it as a vital replacement for other heavies that are getting more scarce or unreliable like those from Mexico, Venezuela or California's Kern River basin. "If they're not available, we need another option," says Zupan. The oil sands, "is where the heavy crude is coming from."

The U.S. would be stupid not to take full advantage of this reliable oil supply to the north.

Pipelines Remain the Safest Way

Enviros are worried about spills and the environment, and that is a fair concern given recent mishaps. But pipelines remain by far the safest way of moving oil. According to the Department of Transportation's pipeline safety division:

Pipelines are the safest and most cost-effective means to transport the extraordinary volumes of natural gas and hazardous liquid products that fuel our economy. To move the volume of even a modest pipeline, it would take a constant line of tanker trucks, about 750 per day, loading up and moving out every two minutes, 24 hours a day, seven days a week. The railroad-equivalent of this single pipeline would be a train of seventy-five 2,000-barrel tank rail cars everyday. These alternatives would require many times the people, clog the air with engine pollutants, be prohibitively expensive and—with many more vehicles on roads and rails carrying hazardous materials—unacceptably dangerous.

According to Dept. of Transportation data, pipelines carrying hazardous liquids average less than 1 hazmat incident for every billion ton miles. That compares with 20.5 incidents per billion ton miles for rail transport and 650 incidents for trucks.

Besides, it's not as if blocking construction of Keystone is making Canada rethink whether or not it wants to develop the oil sands. "Canada is a separate country and they're not real hip on getting lectured to by the U.S. on what they should do with their country," says McGill. "The government of Canada looks at the rejection of Keystone XL and figures, 'we need another market,'" says McGill.

Enbridge has already been working on that. For a decade it has been planning its Northern Gateway line west to the coast of British Columbia. The project has the support of Canada's Prime Minister Stephen Harper. In April, Harper said of President Obama's rejection of Keystone XL: "Look, the very fact that a 'no' could even be said underscores to our country that we must diversify our energy export markets," Harper said.

"We cannot be, as a country, in a situation where our one and, in many cases, only energy partner could say no to our energy products. We just cannot be in that position."

Seeking First Nations Buy-in

Enbridge says it's been working to smooth the path of the Northern Gateway by offering the "First Nations" tribes between the oil sands and the Pacific coast a 10% equity stake in the $5 billion-plus pipeline, a stake that would generate generous dividends for decades to come. Enbridge says it has garnered support of 60% of the tribes living near the path of the line. Critics dispute that and say no pipeline is worth threatening salmon, seals, bears, whales, eagles, rivers and forests.

> *Bakken oil is light and low in sulfur and very easy to refine. Oil sands stuff is very thick, almost asphalty.*

Who knows if Northern Gateway will get built, but as McGill says, "Oil sands is a 150-year resource with 185 billion barrels of recoverable reserves. We've got time. You've got to have patience."

Meanwhile, Enbridge is also heavily involved in the second-biggest boom spot—the Bakken formation of North Dakota.

Bakken oil is very different from the diluted bitumen that comes out of the oil sands. Bakken oil is light and low in sulfur and very easy to refine. Oil sands stuff is very thick, almost asphalty. As a result, even though oil sands pipelines pass pretty close to the North Dakota and Montana home of the Bakken, Enbridge says it can't load Bakken oil into the system that carries bitumen. "There's two different markets, light and heavy," says Leon.

And drilling in the Bakken is ramping up fast. From just 300,000 bpd in 2010, North Dakota is set to surpass both California (540,000 bpd) and Alaska (555,000 bpd) this year to be the second-most oil producing state after Texas. And they've only just gotten started. Myriad analysts predict the Bakken to hit 1 million bpd within five years.

A Transportation Bottleneck

Enbridge has expanded its Bakken pipelines seven times in as many years and still can't keep up with demand. Until it can complete its next $1 billion expansion, the company is building a rail loading terminal that can get 80,000 bpd out of the region.

Moving oil by rail is not only less safe, but far more expensive than pipelines—about $8 per barrel versus $2 by pipeline.

Yet buyers are still willing to pay that extra freight, because bottlenecked Bakken drillers are willing to sell their oil cheap. Enbridge says that among refiners that process light crude, the St. James refinery near New Orleans has recently been buying Bakken crude for a $29 discount relative to the price it would otherwise have to pay for Louisiana Light Sweet crude (a benchmark crude that usually goes for slight premium to West Texas Intermediate). Even after paying the rail freight, St. James is getting cheap oil.

This is a market inefficiency that will only last until more pipelines are built to get more crude to market, at more reasonable (i.e. higher) prices.

All told the new lines could add more than 1.5 million barrels of new daily oil deliveries to the gulf refineries— all of it from North American fields.

This was the rationale behind Enbridge and rival pipeline giant Enterprise Products Partners teaming up last year to buy the Seaway pipeline from ConocoPhillips for $1.2 billion. Conoco had for years been using Seaway to move crude from the Gulf Coast north to Gushing, Okla. But this was the opposite of what the market needed, and only worsened the bottlenecks. Oil producers throughout the mid-continent naturally pleaded with Conoco to reverse Seaway, but it refused, saying a reversal would cost too much (besides, Conoco's midwestern refineries profited from the cheap bottled up crude).

Enbridge and Enterprise have already reversed Seaway to move 150,000 bpd of oil south to the gulf. The companies expect to "twin" the Seaway pipe to carry 400,000 bpd by the end of 2013, and then expand it again, perhaps to as much as 850,000 bpd.

TransCanada, which doesn't need that elusive White House approval to build the lower stretch of the Keystone from Cushing to the gulf, expects that line to add 700,000 bpd of capacity.

All told the new lines could add more than 1.5 million barrels of new daily oil deliveries to the gulf refineries—all of it from North American fields. The Enbridge guys aren't worried a bit about competition from Keystone. Says Zupan, "There's so much production growth going on that there's room for both of us."

It's Time for Honesty About Oil Use

These aren't the kind of guys who worry too much about the effect of oil sands development on global warming. "Oil sands represents 1% of greenhouse gas emissions," says Zupan. "Even if we produced all of it today it would raise the global temperature by .6 degrees over 50 years," says Zupan.

It doesn't matter if that's accurate, where Zupan got his numbers from, or whether .6 degrees is really a lot or a little. Of course pipeline companies are of the opinion that moving more oil and gas is better. (Do you ask your plumber for advice on how long a shower you should take?)

The U.S. is not going to just stop using oil. And as we continue to be addicted to the stuff we have to be honest about where we get it. Venezuela's heavy oil is no "cleaner" than the stuff from the oil sands. Nigeria's pipelines spring a lot more explosive leaks than America's. Iranian crude supports mullahs that want to wipe out Israel. Russian crude supports Putin's autocracy. Saudi crude backs perhaps the most misogynistic and least free regime in the world. We need them all, for now. But with the massive supply growth from Canada and the Bakken, North America could potentially become self sufficient in oil within 15 years. Shouldn't we try?

More Oil Spills Grim Reminders of Needed Energy Revolution

John Austin

John Austin is a writer for New Republic.

This week we got news the Gulf oil spill was done, finally. Last week another oil pipe broke outside Chicago. This follows the massive "oil-letting" in Michigan that began in late July, when a pipeline run by the same Canadian petroleum company, Enbridge, Inc., broke and poured over 800,000 thousand gallons of crude into the Kalamazoo River.

This drip, drip, drip of oil, just as scenes of the Gulf spill have faded seems sent to remind us—like the ghosts of Christmas past—that at the brink of a brave new world and a needed clean energy revolution, we just can't seem to step across the threshold. Rather we remain mired in a fossil fuel-reliant yesterday—a veritable tar pit for dying industries and communities.

These oil spills should serve as a wake up call (as if we needed another) to get cracking with creation of the clean-tech economy. This spur is particularly needed in the industrial metros of the Great Lakes states. Here, as we first noted, the nation's industrial might took root in the cities that ringed the Great Lakes. Here all the great industries that powered the 20th century were born (steel, chemicals, aviation, and, yes, the automobile). This industrial revolution was literally greased by the simultaneous discovery of oil in Northwestern Pennsylvania and Southern Ontario in the late 1800s. The fossil-fuel based carbon revolution was begun.

Fast forward and our Great Lakes metros are among the most carbon-dependent in the nation, with larger carbon footprints, a heavy reliance on coal-burning power, and with their dependence on cars and an auto-enabled lifestyle—the Midwest states produce a disproportionate 5 percent of the world's greenhouse gases.

These oil spills serve to remind us, that until we change our ways, our reliance on oil, coal burning power, and other fossil fuels comes with big ticket consequences for the Great Lakes.

These oil spills serve to remind us, that until we change our ways, our reliance on oil, coal burning power, and other fossil fuels comes with big ticket consequences for the Great Lakes. These involve consequence we can see—like the dead river outside Kalamazoo. Consequences no less real—but still harder to see and connect to our bad fossil fuel habits—like the spiking water temperatures and lowered Great Lakes levels due to climate change. And consequences we don't see at all— like the lack of new jobs making windmills, or solar panels, or electric cars—because we haven't been serious, or fast-enough, in embracing change.

In this same space I recently noted that the Gulf spill had made an on-again, off-again debate about whether to drill for oil under the Great Lakes—definitely off again.

A few years ago, we argued what our friends in Canada had been eager to point out, that while we move towards energy independence and towards clean energy technologies— there were economic and political benefits in the interim to relying more on "friendly" oil from the fast-growing tar sands and related sources in Western Canada, versus spending our petrodollars to subsidize volatile and outright hostile regimes in the Middle East.

One problem with this strategy, and a concern expressed at the time by some, was the need for new pipelines to move this oil to market in the United States—and concern about whether these pipelines pose a new environmental risk. It appears that they do.

> *Unless and until we seriously embrace and lead the clean energy revolution, we will likely have more spills . . . as we miss the boat of clean-technology invention, discovery, and manufacture.*

So as much as I love friendly Canadians and Canadian oil—I am afraid the problem is oil itself, and us. Unless and until we seriously embrace and lead the clean energy revolution, we will likely have more spills, and potentially fewer new jobs, as we miss the boat of clean-technology invention, discovery, and manufacture.

It's not that we don't have the horses to run the clean energy race. As my colleagues Mark Muro and Jim Duderstadt have ably demonstrated, the research institutions of the Great Lakes have the ability to be the energy innovation crucibles for the next economy.

We just have to get cracking and lead the change. The region that helped create the high-carbon American lifestyle of the last century must pivot to become the source for low-carbon technologies, and new, greener urban infrastructures and communities. Or the communities of the Great Lakes of today will be the saber-toothed tigers of tomorrow—interesting museum pieces embalmed in our own "tar pit" of history.

What BP Doesn't Want You to Know About the 2010 Gulf Spill

Mark Hertsgaard

Mark Hertsgaard is a fellow at the New American Foundation and the author, most recently, of HOT: Living Through the Next Fifty Years on Earth. *This article was reported in partnership with the Investigative Fund at the Nation Institute.*

"It's as safe as Dawn dishwashing liquid." That's what Jamie Griffin says the BP man told her about the smelly, rainbow-streaked gunk coating the floor of the "floating hotel" where Griffin was feeding hundreds of cleanup workers during the BP oil disaster in the Gulf of Mexico. Apparently, the workers were tracking the gunk inside on their boots. Griffin, as chief cook and maid, was trying to clean it. But even boiling water didn't work.

"The BP representative said, 'Jamie, just mop it like you'd mop any other dirty floor,'" Griffin recalls in her Louisiana drawl.

It was the opening weeks of what everyone, echoing President Barack Obama, was calling "the worst environmental disaster in American history." At 9:45 p.m. local time on April 20, 2010, a fiery explosion on the Deepwater Horizon oil rig had killed 11 workers and injured 17. One mile underwater, the Macondo well had blown apart, unleashing a gusher of oil into the gulf. At risk were fishing areas that supplied one third of the seafood consumed in the U.S., beaches from Texas to Florida that drew billions of dollars' worth of tourism to local economies, and Obama's chances of reelection. Republicans were blaming him for mishandling the disaster, his poll numbers were falling, even his 11-year-old daughter was demanding, "Daddy, did you plug the hole yet?"

Griffin did as she was told: "I tried Pine-Sol, bleach, I even tried Dawn on those floors." As she scrubbed, the mix of cleanser and gunk occasionally splashed onto her arms and face.

Within days, the 32-year-old single mother was coughing up blood and suffering constant headaches. She lost her voice. "My throat felt like I'd swallowed razor blades," she says.

Then things got much worse.

Like hundreds, possibly thousands, of workers on the cleanup, Griffin soon fell ill with a cluster of excruciating, bizarre, grotesque ailments. By July, unstoppable muscle spasms were twisting her hands into immovable claws. In August, she began losing her short-term memory. After cooking professionally for 10 years, she couldn't remember the recipe for vegetable soup; one morning, she got in the car to go to work, only to discover she hadn't put on pants. The right side, but only the right side, of her body "started acting crazy. It felt like the nerves were coming out of my skin. It was so painful. My right leg swelled my ankle would get as wide as my calf and my skin got incredibly itchy."

"These are the same symptoms experienced by soldiers who returned from the Persian Gulf War with Gulf War syndrome," says Dr. Michael Robichaux, a Louisiana physician and former state senator, who treated Griffin and 113 other patients with similar complaints. As a general practitioner, Robichaux says he had "never seen this grouping of symptoms together: skin problems, neurological impairments, plus pulmonary problems." Only months later, after Kaye H. Kilburn, a former professor of medicine at the University of Southern California and one of the nation's leading environmental health experts, came to Louisiana and tested 14 of Robichaux's patients did the two physicians make the connection with

Gulf War syndrome, the malady that afflicted an estimated 250,000 veterans of that war with a mysterious combination of fatigue, skin inflammation, and cognitive problems.

BP mounted a cover-up that concealed the full extent of its crimes from public view.

Meanwhile, the well kept hemorrhaging oil. The world watched with bated breath as BP failed in one attempt after another to stop the leak. An agonizing 87 days passed before the well was finally plugged on July 15. By then, 210 million gallons of Louisiana sweet crude had escaped into the Gulf of Mexico, according to government estimates, making the BP disaster the largest accidental oil leak in world history.

In 2010, Pulitzer Prize-winning animator Mark Fiore created this humorous and poignant take on the BP oil spill.

Yet three years later, the BP disaster has been largely forgotten, both overseas and in the U.S. Popular anger has cooled. The media have moved on. Today, only the business press offers serious coverage of what the *Financial Times* calls "the trial of the century"—the trial now under way in New Orleans, where BP faces tens of billions of dollars in potential penalties for the disaster. As for Obama, the same president who early in the BP crisis blasted the "scandalously close relationship" between oil companies and government regulators two years later ran for reelection boasting about how much new oil and gas development his administration had approved.

Such collective amnesia may seem surprising, but there may be a good explanation for it: BP mounted a cover-up that concealed the full extent of its crimes from public view. This cover-up prevented the media and therefore the public from knowing—and above all, seeing—just how much oil was gushing into the gulf. The disaster appeared much less extensive and destructive than it actually was. BP declined to comment for this article.

That BP lied about the amount of oil it discharged into the gulf is already established. Lying to Congress about that was one of 14 felonies to which BP pleaded guilty last year in a legal settlement with the Justice Department that included a $4.5 billion fine, the largest fine ever levied against a corporation in the U.S.

What has not been revealed until now is how BP hid that massive amount of oil from TV cameras and the price that this "disappearing act" imposed on cleanup workers, coastal residents, and the ecosystem of the gulf. That story can now be told because an anonymous whistleblower has provided evidence that BP was warned in advance about the safety risks of attempting to cover up its leaking oil. Nevertheless, BP proceeded. Furthermore, BP appears to have withheld these safety warnings, as well as protective measures, both from the thousands of workers hired for the cleanup and from the millions of Gulf Coast residents who stood to be affected.

The financial implications are enormous. The trial now under way in New Orleans is wrestling with whether BP was guilty of "negligence" or "gross negligence" for the Deepwater Horizon disaster. If found guilty of "negligence," BP would be fined, under the Clean Water Act, $1,100 for each barrel of oil that leaked. But if found guilty of "gross negligence"—which a cover-up would seem to imply BP would be fined $4,300 per barrel, almost four times as much, for a total of $17.5 billion. That large a fine, combined with an additional $34 billion that the states of Louisiana, Alabama, Mississippi, and Florida are seeking, could have a powerful effect on BP's economic health.

Yet the most astonishing thing about BP's cover-up? It was carried out in plain sight, right in front of the world's uncomprehending news media (including, I regret to say, this reporter).

The chief instrument of BPs cover-up was the same substance that apparently sickened Jamie Griffin and countless other cleanup workers and local residents. Its brand name is Corexit, but most news reports at the time referred to it simply as a "dispersant." Its function was to attach itself to leaked oil, break it into droplets, and disperse them into the vast reaches of the gulf, thereby keeping the oil from reaching Gulf Coast shorelines. And the Corexit did largely achieve this goal.

The combination of Corexit and crude oil also caused terrible damage to gulf wildlife and ecosystems, including an unprecedented number of seafood mutations; declines of up to 80 percent in seafood catch; and massive die-offs of the microscopic life-forms.

But the 1.84 million gallons of Corexit that BP applied during the cleanup also served a public-relations purpose: they made the oil spill all but disappear, at least from TV screens. By late July 2010, the *Associated Press* and The *New York Times* were questioning whether the spill had been such a big deal after all. Time went so far as to assert that right-wing talk-radio host Rush Limbaugh "has a point" when he accused journalists and environmentalists of exaggerating the crisis.

But BP had a problem: it had lied about how safe Corexit is, and proof of its dishonesty would eventually fall into the hands of the Government Accountability Project, the premiere whistleblower-protection group in the U.S. The proof? A technical manual BP had received from NALCO, the firm that supplied the Corexit that BP used in the gulf.

An electronic copy of that manual is included in a new report GAP has issued, "Deadly Dispersants in the Gulf." On the basis of interviews with dozens of cleanup workers, scientists, and Gulf Coast residents, GAP concludes that the health impacts endured by Griffin were visited upon many other locals as well. What's more, the combination of Corexit and crude oil also caused terrible damage to gulf wildlife and ecosystems, including an unprecedented number of seafood mutations; declines of up to 80 percent in seafood catch; and massive die-offs of the microscopic life-forms at the base of the marine food chain. GAP warns that BP and the U.S. government nevertheless appear poised to repeat the exercise after the next major oil spill: "As a result of Corexit's perceived success, Corexit . . . has become the dispersant of choice in the U.S. to 'clean up' oil spills."

BP's cover-up was not planned in advance but devised in the heat of the moment as the oil giant scrambled to limit the PR and other damages of the disaster. Indeed, one of the chief scandals of the disaster is just how unprepared both BP and federal and state authorities were for an oil leak of this magnitude. U.S. law required that a response plan be in place before drilling began, but the plan was embarrassingly flawed.

"We weren't managing for actual risk; we were checking a box," says Mark Davis, director of the Institute on Water Resources Law and Policy at Tulane University. "That's how we ended up with a response plan that included provisions for dealing with the impacts to walruses: because [BP] copied word for word the response plans that had been developed after the Exxon-Valdez oil spill [in Alaska, in 1989] instead of a plan tailored to the conditions in the gulf."

As days turned into weeks and it became obvious that no one knew how to plug the gushing well, BP began insisting that Corexit be used to disperse the leaking oil. This triggered alarms from scientists and from a leading environmental NGO in Louisiana, the Louisiana Environmental Action Network (LEAN).

The group's scientific adviser, Wilma Subra, a chemist whose work on environmental pollution had won her a "genius grant" from the MacArthur Foundation, told state and federal authorities that she was especially concerned about how dangerous the mixture of crude and Corexit was: "The short-term health symptoms include acute respiratory problems, skin rashes, cardiovascular impacts, gastrointestinal impacts, and short-term loss of memory," she told GAP investigators. "Long-term impacts include cancer, decreased lung function, liver damage, and kidney damage."

(Nineteen months after the Deepwater Horizon explosion, a scientific study published in the peer-reviewed journal Environmental Pollution found that crude oil becomes 52 times more toxic when combined with Corexit.)

BP even rebuffed a direct request from the administrator of the Environmental Protection Agency, Lisa Jackson, who wrote BP a letter on May 19, asking the company to deploy a less toxic dispersant in the cleanup. Jackson could only ask BP to do this; she could not legally require it. Why? Because use of Corexit had been authorized years before under the federal Oil Pollution Act.

In a recent interview, Jackson explains that she and other officials "had to determine, with less-than-perfect scientific testing and data, whether use of dispersants would, despite potential side effects, improve the overall situation in the gulf and coastal ecosystems. The tradeoff, as I have said many times, was potential damage in the deep water versus the potential for larger amounts of undispersed oil in the ecologically rich coastal shallows and estuaries." She adds that the presidential commission that later studied the BP oil disaster did not fault the decision to use dispersants.

Knowing that EPA lacked the authority to stop it, BP wrote back to Jackson on May 20, declaring that Corexit was safe. What's more, BP wrote, there was a ready supply of Corexit, which was not the case with alternative dispersants. (A NALCO plant was located just 30 miles west of New Orleans.)

But Corexit was decidedly not safe without taking proper precautions, as the manual BP got from NALCO spelled out in black and white. The "Vessel Captains Hazard Communication" resource manual, which GAP shared with me, looks innocuous enough. A three-ring binder with a black plastic cover, the manual contained 61 sheets, each wrapped in plastic, that detailed the scientific properties of the two types of Corexit that BP was buying, as well as their health hazards and recommended measures against those hazards.

BP applied two types of Corexit in the gulf. The first, Corexit 9527, was considerably more toxic. According to the NALCO manual, Corexit 9527 is an "eye and skin irritant. Repeated or excessive exposure . . . may cause injury to red blood cells (hemolysis), kidney or the liver." The manual adds: "Excessive exposure may cause central nervous system effects, nausea, vomiting, anesthetic or narcotic effects." It advises, "Do not get in eyes, on skin, on clothing," and "Wear suitable protective clothing."

Misrepresenting the safety of Corexit went hand in hand with BP's previously noted lie about how much oil was leaking from the Macondo well.

When available supplies of Corexit 9527 were exhausted early in the cleanup, BP switched to the second type of dispersant, Corexit 9500. In its recommendations for dealing with Corexit 9500, the NALCO manual advised, "Do not get in eyes, on skin, on clothing," "Avoid breathing vapor," and "Wear suitable protective clothing."

It's standard procedure—and required by U.S. law—for companies to distribute this kind of information to any work site where hazardous materials are present so workers can know about the dangers they face and how to protect themselves. But interviews with numerous cleanup workers suggest that this legally required precaution was rarely if ever followed during the BP cleanup. Instead, it appears that BP told NALCO to stop including the manuals with the Corexit that NALCO was delivering to cleanup work sites.

"It's my understanding that some manuals were sent out with the shipments of Corexit in the beginning [of the cleanup]," the anonymous source tells me. "Then, BP told

NALCO to stop sending them. So NALCO was left with a roomful of unused binders."

Roman Blahoski, NALCO's director of global communications, says: "NALCO responded to requests for its pre-approved dispersants from those charged with protecting the gulf and mitigating the environmental, health, and economic impact of this event. NALCO was never involved in decisions relating to the use, volume, and application of its dispersant."

Misrepresenting the safety of Corexit went hand in hand with BP's previously noted lie about how much oil was leaking from the Macondo well. As reported by John Rudolf in The Huffington Post, internal BP emails show that BP privately estimated that "the runaway well could be leaking from 62,000 barrels a day to 146,000 barrels a day." Meanwhile, BP officials were telling the government and the media that only 5,000 barrels a day were leaking.

In short, applying Corexit enabled BP to mask the fact that a much larger amount of oil was actually leaking into the gulf. "Like any good magician, the oil industry has learned that if you can't see something that was there, it must have 'disappeared,'" Scott Porter, a scientist and deep-sea diver who consults for oil companies and oystermen, says in the GAP report. "Oil companies have also learned that, in the public mind, 'out of sight equals out of mind.' Therefore, they have chosen crude oil dispersants as the primary tool for handling large marine oil spills."

BP also had a more direct financial interest in using Corexit, argues Clint Guidry, president of the Louisiana Shrimp Association, whose members include not only shrimpers but fishermen of all sorts. As it happens, local fishermen constituted a significant portion of BP's cleanup force (which numbered as many as 47,000 workers at the height of the cleanup). Because the spill caused the closure of their fishing grounds, BP and state and federal authorities established the Vessels of Opportunity (VoO) program, in which BP paid fishermen to take their boats out and skim, burn, and otherwise get rid of leaked oil. Applying dispersants, Guidry points out, reduced the total volume of oil that could be traced back to BP.

"The next phase of this trial [against BP] is going to turn on how much oil was leaked," Guidry tells me. [If found guilty, BP will be fined a certain amount for each barrel of oil judged to have leaked.] "So hiding the oil with Corexit worked not only to hide the size of the spill but also to lower the amount of oil that BP may get charged for releasing."

Not only did BP fail to inform workers of the potential hazards of Corexit and to provide them with safety training and protective gear, according to interviews with dozens of cleanup workers, the company also allegedly threatened to fire workers who complained about the lack of respirators and protective clothing.

"I worked with probably a couple hundred different fishermen on the [cleanup]," Acy Cooper, Guidry's second in command, tells me in Venice, the coastal town from which many VoO vessels departed. "Not one of them got any safety information or training concerning the toxic materials they encountered." Cooper says that BP did provide workers with body suits and gloves designed for handling hazardous materials. "But when I'd talk with [the BP representative] about getting my guys respirators and air monitors, I'd never get any response."

Roughly 58 percent of the 1.84 million gallons of Corexit used in the cleanup was sprayed onto the gulf from C-130 airplanes. The spray sometimes ended up hitting cleanup workers in the face.

"Our boat was sprayed four times," says Jorey Danos, a 32-year-old father of three who suffered racking coughing fits, severe fatigue, and memory loss after working on the BP cleanup. "I could see the stuff coming out of the plane like a shower of mist, a smoky color. I could see [it] coming at me, but there was nothing I could do."

"The next day," Danos continues, "when the BP rep came around on his speed boat, I asked, 'Hey, what's the deal with that stuff that was coming out of those planes yesterday?' He told me, 'Don't worry about it.' I said, 'Man, that s--t was burning my face it ain't right.' He said, 'Don't worry about it.' I said, 'Well, could we get some respirators or something, because that s--t is bad.' He said, 'No, that wouldn't look good to the media. You got two choices: you can either be relieved of your duties or you can deal with it.'"

Perhaps the single most hazardous chemical compound found in Corexit 9527 is 2-Butoxyethanol, a substance that had been linked to cancers and other health impacts among cleanup workers on the 1989 Exxon-Valdez oil spill in Alaska. According to BP's own data, 20 percent of offshore workers in the gulf had levels of 2-Butoxyethanol two times higher than the level certified as safe by the Occupational Safety and Health Administration.

Cleanup workers were not the only victims; coastal residents also suffered. "My 2-year-old grandson and I would play out in the yard," says Shirley Tillman of the Mississippi coastal town Pass Christian. "You could smell oil and stuff in the air, but on the news they were saying it's fine, don't worry. Well, by October, he was one sick little fellow. All of a sudden, this very active little 2-year-old was constantly sick. He was having headaches, upper respiratory infections, earaches. The night of his birthday party, his parents had to rush him to the emergency room. He went to nine different doctors, but they treated just the symptoms; they're not toxicologists."

"It's not the crime, it's the cover-up." Ever since the Watergate scandal of the 1970s, that's been the mantra. Cover-ups don't work, goes the argument. They only dig a deeper hole, because the truth eventually comes out.

But does it?

GAP investigators were hopeful that obtaining the NALCO manual might persuade BP to meet with them, and it did. On

July 10, 2012, BP hosted a private meeting at its Houston offices. Presiding over the meeting, which is described here publicly for the first time, was BP's public ombudsman, Stanley Sporkin, joining by telephone from Washington. Ironically, Sporkin had made his professional reputation during the Watergate scandal. As a lawyer with the Securities and Exchange Commission, Sporkin investigated illegal corporate payments to the slush fund that President Nixon used to buy the silence of the Watergate burglars.

Also attending the meeting were two senior BP attorneys; BP Vice President Luke Keller; other BP officials; Thomas Devine, GAP's senior attorney on the BP case; Shanna Devine, GAP's investigator on the case; Dr. Michael Robichaux; Dr. Wilma Subra; and Marylee Orr, the executive director of LEAN. The following account is based on my interviews with Thomas Devine, Robichaux, Subra, and Orr. BP declined to comment.

BP officials had previously confirmed the authenticity of the NALCO manual, says Thomas Devine, but now they refused to discuss it, even though this had been one of the stated purposes for the meeting. Nor would BP address the allegation, made by the whistleblower who had given the manual to GAP, that BP had ordered the manual withheld from cleanup work sites, perhaps to maintain the fiction that Corexit was safe.

BP's cover-up of the gulf oil disaster speaks to the enormous power that giant corporations exercise in modern society, and how unable, or unwilling, governments are to limit that power.

"They opened the meeting with this upbeat presentation about how seriously they took their responsibilities for the spill and all the wonderful things they were doing to make things right," says Devine. "When it was my turn to speak, I said that the manual our whistleblower had provided contradicted what they just said. I asked whether they had ordered the manual withdrawn from work sites. Their attorneys said that was a matter they would not discuss because of the pending litigation on the spill." [Disclosure: Thomas Devine is a friend of this reporter.]

The visitors'top priority was to get BP to agree not to use Corexit in the future. Keller said that Corexit was still authorized for use by the U.S. government and BP would indeed feel free to use it against any future oil spills.

A second priority was to get BP to provide medical treatment for Jamie Griffin and the many other apparent victims of Corexit-and-crude poisoning. This request too was refused by BP.

Robichaux doubts his patients will receive proper compensation from the $7.8 billion settlement BP reached in 2012 with the Plaintiffs'Steering Committee, 19 court-appointed attorneys who represent the hundreds of individuals and entities that have sued BP for damages related to the gulf disaster. "Nine of the most common symptoms of my patients do not appear on the list of illnesses that settlement says can be compensated, including memory loss, fatigue, and joint and muscular pain," says Robichaux. "So how are the attorneys going to file suits on behalf of those victims?"

At one level, BP's cover-up of the gulf oil disaster speaks to the enormous power that giant corporations exercise in modern society, and how unable, or unwilling, governments are to limit that power. To be sure, BP has not entirely escaped censure for its actions; depending on the outcome of the trial now under way in New Orleans, the company could end up paying tens of billions of dollars in fines and damages over and above the $4.5 billion imposed by the Justice Department in the settlement last year. But BP's reputation appears to have survived: its market value as this article went to press was a tidy $132 billion, and few, if any, BP officials appear likely to face any legal repercussions. "If I would have killed 11 people, I'd be hanging from a noose," says Jorey Danos. "Not BP. It's the golden rule: the man with the gold makes the rules."

As unchastened as anyone at BP is Bob Dudley, the American who was catapulted into the CEO job a few weeks into the gulf disaster to replace Tony Hayward, whose propensity for imprudent comments—"I want my life back," the multimillionaire had pouted while thousands of gulf workers and residents were suffering—had made him a globally derided figure. Dudley told the annual BP shareholders meeting in London last week that Corexit "is effectively . . . dishwashing soap," no more toxic than that, as all scientific studies supposedly showed. What's more, Dudley added, he himself had grown up in Mississippi and knows that the Gulf of Mexico is "an ecosystem that is used to oil."

Nor has the BP oil disaster triggered the kind of changes in law and public priorities one might have expected. "Not much has actually changed," says Mark Davis of Tulane. "It reflects just how wedded our country is to keeping the Gulf of Mexico producing oil and bringing it to our shores as cheaply as possible. Going forward, no one should assume that just because something really bad happened we're going to manage oil and gas production with greater sensitivity and wisdom. That will only happen if people get involved and compel both the industry and the government to be more diligent."

And so the worst environmental disaster in U.S. history has been whitewashed—its true dimensions obscured, its victims forgotten, its lessons ignored. Who says cover-ups never work?

The Economic Benefits of Arctic Oil Are Not Worth the Environmental Risk

Greenpeace International

Founded in 1971, Greenpeace International is an international organization that uses peaceful direct action and creative communication to address global environmental problems.

Arctic oil drilling is a dangerous, high-risk enterprise and an oil spill under these icy waters would have a catastrophic impact on one of the most pristine, unique and beautiful landscapes on earth. The risks of such an accident are ever present and the oil industry's response plans remain wholly inadequate.

The Arctic's extreme weather and freezing temperatures, its remote location and the presence of moving sea ice severely increase the risks of oil drilling, complicate logistics and present unparalleled difficulties for any clean-up operation. Its fragile ecosystem is particularly vulnerable to an oil spill and the consequences of an accident would have a profound effect on the environment and local fisheries.

The Arctic is home to four million people, many of whom are descendants of Indigenous communities who have lived in the Far North for thousands of years. It also houses a diverse range of unique wildlife: hundreds of species of seabirds, millions of migrating birds; 17 different species of whale live there, while experts believe that 90% of the world's narwhal population can be found in Baffin Bay alone. Mammals including Polar Bears, Arctic Foxes and various species of seal inhabit the Arctic at different points throughout the year. The impact of a spill on these communities and already vulnerable animal species would be devastating and long-lasting.

The US Geological Survey estimates that around 13% of the world's undiscovered oil could lie under the area north of the Arctic Circle. Sounds like a lot? At our current oil consumption rate, that's actually only three years' worth of resources.

In the Arctic's freezing conditions, oil is known to behave very differently than in lower latitudes.

Due to climate change, the Arctic sea ice is melting at an alarming rate each summer, allowing creeping industrialisation as companies and governments scramble for the region's natural resources.

Drilling Challenges Are Formidable

However, drilling in the Arctic presents, as even Cairn Energy admits, "significant challenges." Alongside the logistical nightmare of operating in such a hostile and remote region, oil rigs face an ever-present risk from huge icebergs and have to employ fleets of ships to drag them out of the way. Some of the icebergs are so big, though, that oil rigs are forced to stop drilling and move out of their way.

The Arctic drilling season is limited to a narrow window of a few months during the summer. In this short period of time, completing the huge logistical response needed to cap a leaking well would be almost impossible. For instance, the successful drilling of vital relief wells, crucial to permanently capping a reptured well, could not be guaranteed before the winter ice returns. If relief wells are left unfinished over the winter, oil could continue to gush out for up to two years. Yet despite these incredible risks, oil companies continue to recklessly lobby governments to relax Arctic drilling safety rules.

Spill Damage in Arctic Would Persist

In the Arctic's freezing conditions, oil is known to behave very differently than in lower latitudes. It takes much longer to disperse in cold water and experts suggest that there is no way to contain or clean-up oil trapped underneath large bodies of ice. Toxic traces would linger for a longer period, affecting local wildlife for longer, be transported large distances by ice floes and leave a lasting stain on this pristine environment.

The closest example we have seen of the effects of an oil spill in these Northern extremes is the *Exxon Valdez* tanker spill in Alaska. Two decades later, the region is still suffering the after-effects, with local populations of otters being severely harmed, orcas yet to recover and spilled oil remaining in areas on land. The impact of a blow-out on the Arctic seabed could be far more significant for the waters of the High North.

The oil industry has demonstrated time and time again that it is simply not prepared to deal with the risks and consequences of drilling in the Arctic. One senior official from a Canadian firm that specializes in oil-spill response openly stated that: "There is really no solution or method today that we're aware of that can actually recover [spilled] oil from the Arctic."

We hear that Shell is also paying to train Dachshunds to hunt out oil trapped under thick layers of ice.

Response Plans Are Inadequate

Yet Shell claimed it could clean up 95% of a possible spill in the Beaufort, a fantastical figure when you consider that the US Geological Survey thinks only 1–20% could be recovered from an Arctic spill, while recovery rates from the *Exxon Valdez* spill were estimated to be 9% and only 17% for *Deepwater Horizon*.

Cairn's oil spill response plan, eventually made public after months of pressure from Greenpeace, is, as oil spill expert Rick Steiner underlined, wholly inadequate. So-called "solutions" like transporting blocks of contaminated ice to warehouses and letting them melt to recover the oil, or claims that fish have been found to swim away from oil (which experts have shown is simply not true), are outlandish and unrealistic.

Shell's spill response plan for an accident in the Chukchi Sea was recently approved by the US government. This document is supposed to explain what Shell will do to block a ruptured well and save this Arctic region from an ecological catastrophe, but even a quick read shows that the company would be entirely unable to respond to an accident in the High North. In fact, it's more like a negligence plan than a spill plan, depending on a capping and containment system that hasn't even been built, on deflection barriers that will not work properly in ice and with on-shore clean-up plans that look like they've been drawn by children. At the same time we hear that Shell is also paying to train Dachshunds to hunt out oil trapped under thick layers of ice.

No Guarantee of Safety

All we need to do is look at BP's response to the Gulf of Mexico oil spill to realize how challenging Arctic drilling could be. The company needed over 6,000 ships, more than 50,000 people and a massive cheque book to cap its leaking well, and even then it didn't manage it for months, causing the biggest environmental disaster in US history. If Big Oil cannot adequately respond to a spill in temperate conditions near to large population centers and with the best response resources available, how can we be assured by claims that they are prepared to deal with a spill in the extreme Arctic environment? A top US Coast Guard's official recently admitted that they currently have "zero" spill response capability in the Arctic.

The oil industry cannot guarantee the safety of Arctic drilling and is recklessly putting profit before the environment. As Cairn's recent operations prove, the immense technical, economic and environmental risks of drilling in the Arctic just aren't worth it.

CHAPTER 3

Is the Oil Industry Prepared to Handle Major Oil Spills?

Chapter Preface

According to the American Petroleum Institute (API), the national trade association for the oil and natural gas industry, "today, more than 99.9995% of the oil produced, refined, stored and/or transported in the United States reaches its destination safely and without incident."

But it is the other tiny fraction of a percent that makes global headlines and generates so much concern for the environment.

There is little disagreement that British Petroleum (BP) was unprepared to handle the massive *Deepwater Horizon* spill in the Gulf of Mexico in 2010. Because of the extreme depth and pressure, the well spewed more than two hundred million gallons of oil for an unprecedented eighty-seven days before it was finally capped. Engineers were ill-prepared to make repairs under such extreme conditions, and they encountered unanticipated problems. Several attempts to cap the blown well failed, and the effort to bring the well under control was truly a trial and error process. In congressional hearings after the disaster, government leaders slammed BP executives for their risk-taking and pointed fingers at other oil companies as well, saying the whole industry suffered from a lack of preparedness.

As devastating as the Gulf spill was, some say it was also a positive turning point for the oil industry. Industry leaders maintain that the *Deepwater Horizon* event ultimately made the industry better and safer because it served as a wake-up call to improve safety practices and spill preparedness industry-wide.

"Learning from the past is essential to creating a future that keeps oil out of the environment and producing energy for Americans," the API says on its website. "In the wake of the Gulf of Mexico spill of 2010, our industry launched a comprehensive review of our offshore operations and safety procedures."

Indeed, the industry now boasts of having "one of the world's most sophisticated and well-coordinated spill response networks, bringing together the resources and expertise of private industry, public agencies and academia."

API goes on to say that "every community in the United States is linked into a coordinated network of expertise and technical resources (known as the National Response System) prepared to respond quickly and effectively to incidents of any size."

Every oil spill is different, and the type of oil, the size of the spill, and where the spill takes place are all factors that work together to determine what sort of cleanup is needed or even possible. For example, heavy tar sands oil that spills from a breached pipeline into a nearby river presents quite different environmental concerns and cleanup challenges than a spill of light crude oil from a tanker far out at sea, or than heavy crude washing up on beaches or coating birds in a coastal marsh. Oil companies now rely on a new tool called Net Environmental Benefit Analysis (NEBA) to systematically evaluate conditions and decide on protocols for how to best respond to a particular spill.

Aside from the organizational, informational, technical, and logistic improvements in the industry overall since the Gulf disaster, API points to other areas of improvement as well, such as sophisticated monitoring systems for pipelines and storage tanks that detect weak spots so they can be repaired before leaks develop, and redesigned tankers that can withstand accidents and thereby prevent spills (by 2015, all tankers operating in US waters will be double-hulled.)

But while industry critics agree that preventing spills in the first place is better than cleaning them up, they still maintain that the oil industry remains woefully unprepared to properly clean up major spills, especially in today's more extreme drilling environments. As the industry has expanded its operations to new environments and adopted new extraction technologies, new variables are increasingly coming into play. Today's extreme drilling conditions—such as *Deepwater Horizon*'s unprecedented depth and pressure, or the Arctic where subzero temperatures change the way that oil behaves and where sea ice can hamper spill responders and equipment—are bringing new risks, challenges, and complications that many say cannot be fully anticipated.

Perhaps the most ironic thing about oil spills is that only by them happening under new and various conditions are erroneous assumptions and inadequacies in safety and response planning revealed. Every time a new spill happens under new conditions and with new results, scientists and oil industry leaders learn more about best practices for cleanup and restoration and they gain a better understanding of the long-term effects of oil spills on the environment. And, most importantly, they learn more about how to prevent such spills in the first place. For environmental groups, though, an oil spill endangering pristine environments and wildlife is simply too big a risk to justify drilling in the first place.

The authors in this chapter present differing views about whether the oil industry is prepared to clean up future spills, and whether the steep learning curve of dealing with the consequences of new extraction environments and technologies is worth the risk.

The Oil Industry Is Committed to Spill Prevention and Response

Chris Kahn

Chris Kahn is a former energy writer and reporter for The Associated Press. He is now an editor at the online financial website bankrate.com.

A group of oil companies led by Exxon said Thursday [February 2011] that they have a system that can stop an undersea oil spill within weeks, a critical step towards resuming drilling in the deepest parts of the Gulf of Mexico.

The Marine Well Containment Co. says it has cobbled together enough equipment and support vessels to contain a spill similar to BP's massive gusher, which took 85 days to plug. Some of the equipment was used by BP.

Regulators have demanded that oil companies demonstrate the capability to contain a blowout of an underwater well before granting permits to drill in Gulf waters deeper than 500 feet (152 meters).

Exxon said this system, available immediately, meets that demand and should have no trouble gaining government approval. Its engineers consulted with regulators during the system's development.

"They've been looking at the system all along," said Clay Vaughn, an ExxonMobil vice president who is supervising the response network. In an interview with The Associated Press, Vaughn said officials observed tests of the equipment Wednesday.

Shell Offshore, a member of the Exxon group, is first in line for a new deepwater permit. The government has until the end of the month to decide whether to approve Shell's Garden Banks project, about 137 miles (220 kilometers) from the Louisiana coast.

Drilling was suspended last year when the Obama administration imposed a moratorium after the BP spill. The ban was lifted in October, but drilling has not yet resumed in Gulf waters deeper than 500 feet.

The system is designed to be fully assembled two to three weeks after a blowout. The group says it should handle blowouts at 8,000 feet (2,438 meters) underwater and capture as much as 60,000 barrels of liquid and 120 million cubic feet of natural gas per day. BP's Macondo well blew out at a depth of about 5,000 feet (1,524 meters) and spilled about 52,400 barrels per day.

The containment system will look like the network BP eventually used last summer to stop its spill. Only this time the industry has had months to perfect it.

A more robust system that can collect more oil and operate at greater depths is expected to be finished early next year.

Michael Bromwich, director of the Bureau of Ocean Energy Management, Regulation and Enforcement, said earlier this month that he wouldn't open the Gulf to deepwater drilling until companies showed they had "access to and the ability to deploy" equipment that can contain another spill.

Exxon, Chevron, Shell and ConocoPhillips agreed in July to pool $1 billion and form a company that could respond to an offshore oil spill at up to 10,000 feet (3,048 meters) in an effort to show Washington the industry is capable of handling another deepwater disaster. BP has since joined the group.

The containment system will look like the network BP eventually used last summer to stop its spill. Only this time the industry has had months to perfect it.

"Everything BP did was on the fly," Exxon spokesman Alan Jeffers said. "Our engineers have had a lot of time to think about how to get this right."

The system relies on a variety of well-plugging equipment scattered throughout the Gulf.

If another well experiences an uncontrolled blowout, drillers can alert staff at the containment company's headquarters in Houston. Within 24 hours, the company will start moving equipment and vessels.

In Houston, crews will dispatch a 100-ton stack of steel valves known as the containment assembly. This can either plug the well at the sea floor or funnel oil and gas to the surface through manifolds, risers and flow lines donated by BP from last year's operation. Drill ships on loan from Chevron and BP will arrive to gather and dispose of liquid from the well.

Next year, when the group presents an expanded network capable of plugging a well more than 10,000 feet (3,048 meters) below the surface, it's expected to handle 100,000 barrels of liquid and 200 million cubic feet of gas per day.

One of the main weaknesses of the new response system is that it can handle only one spill at a time. While major spills are extremely rare, it still raises the question of what would happen if multiple disasters happened at once. There were about three dozen deepwater drilling projects underway last year before the government shut them down.

Vaughn contends oil spills should never happen. Exxon and its partners built the response network mostly as an insurance policy.

"The view was that we couldn't afford to not have a rapidly deployable response system," he said. "And we're ready for business."

Cleaning Up Oil Spills With Magnets and Nanotechnology

Tom Levitt

Tom Levitt is currently a managing editor at China Dialogue whose journalistic work has been featured in such media outlets as CNN, the Guardian, and the Independent.

Oil companies could soon be using an innovative new technique involving nanotechnology and magnets to help clean up offshore oil spills.

Oil spills from container ships or offshore platforms are a frequent hazard to marine and coastal ecosystems and an expensive one to clean up. BP expects the Gulf of Mexico oil spill in 2010—the worst environmental disaster in U.S. history—to cost it $40 billion.

However, researchers from the Massachusetts Institute of Technology (MIT) say they have found a method of recovering oil after a spill using magnets, potentially saving companies like BP money in clean up bills.

On it's own, oil is not magnetic, but MIT researchers say that when mixed with water-repellent nanoparticles that contain iron, the oil can be magnetically separated from the water. The nanoparticles can later be removed to enable the reuse of the oil.

"I had known about other scientists using magnetic fluids to separate oil but it had never worked out practically and that was something I felt I could do something about," says co-researcher Markus Zahn.

The recovery process would be conducted out at sea after the oil spill, explains Zahn. Seawater polluted with oil would be pumped onto a boat treatment facility. Once onboard, the magnetic nanoparticles would be added and attach themselves to the oil.

The liquid would then be filtered with the magnets to separate the oil and water, with the water returned to the sea and the oil carried back to shore to an oil refinery.

"I think in the world we are in, there are always going to be spillages which affect the wildlife and livelihoods of people and this can help tackle that," says Zahn.

Since the 2010 Gulf of Mexico oil spill, there has been a rise in interest from oil companies and government departments in funding new techniques for reducing the environmental impact and cost of future oil spills.

The use of tiny nanoparticles is seen by some as controversial. . . . There are concerns they could damage marine life, if accidentally released.

Until now the two main methods have been using chemical dispersants, which break up the oil, and skimming, a technique whereby the oil is pulled off the surface of the water.

Although there are drawbacks to both—chemical dispersants can have negative impacts on marine life and skimming can be hampered by bad weather—magnetic techniques may still find it difficult to gain acceptance.

Zahn admits that one oil company has already turned down the opportunity of funding the research but is confident that other companies will support the project.

The use of tiny nanoparticles is seen by some as controversial. As well as being complex and difficult to use on a large-scale, there are concerns they could damage marine life, if accidentally released.

While their impact on the environment is still largely un-known, scientists such as David Andrews from the U.S.-based Environmental Working Group (EWG), say their use should be limited.

Others suggest the magnetic technique would be better suited to small-scale use and that existing alternatives such as skimming are still better suited for tackling large-scale off-shore oil spills.

"On a small-scale it (the magnetic technique) may be an excellent system but I don't think it will work at sea in such a challenging environment," says Dr Susan Shaw, founder of the Marine Environmental Research Institute.

"I think ultimately, it may be a better way of recovering oil once it is brought ashore rather than out at sea."

For Shaw, a newly developed skimmer from an Illinois company Team Elastic offers a better method for cleaning up oil spills. It can recover about 4,700 gallons per minute, so as-suming the skimmer could be deployed 24 hours a day, it would take 30 days to pick up the entire 200 million gallons of oil spilled during the Gulf of Mexico disaster.

"In my opinion, the new skimmers are the most hopeful and best method for cleaning up an oil spill and protecting health and the environment. They should be part of the safety equipment required by permit for every offshore drilling rig," says Shaw.

The Oil Industry Is Unprepared to Handle Spills in the Arctic

Suzanne Goldenberg

Suzanne Goldenberg is the US environment correspondent for The Guardian *newspaper in the United Kingdom.*

The next big offshore oil disaster could take place in the remote Arctic seas where hurricane-force winds, 30ft seas, sub-zero temperatures and winter darkness would overwhelm any clean-up attempts, a new report warns.

With the ban on offshore drilling lifted in the Gulf of Mexico, big oil companies such as Royal Dutch Shell are pressing hard for the [Barack] Obama administration to grant final approval to Arctic drilling. Shell has invested more than $2bn [billion] to drill off Alaska's north coast, and is campaigning to begin next summer [2011].

But the report, "Oil Spill Prevention and Response in the US Arctic Ocean", by the Pew Environment Group, warns that oil companies are not ready to deal with a spill, despite the lessons of the BP disaster in the Gulf of Mexico.

"There is a lot of pressure by Shell to drill this summer," Marilyn Heiman, director of the US Arctic programme at Pew said. "But the oil companies are just not prepared for the Arctic. The spill plans are thoroughly inadequate."

It took BP three months to bring its ruptured well under control. The former chief executive, Tony Hayward, admitted this week that the company had to improvise its response plan as it went along.

Arctic Spill Would Present Extreme Challenges

Trying to clean up a spill in the extreme conditions of the Arctic would be on an entirely different order of magnitude. "The risks, difficulties, and unknowns of oil exploration in the Arctic . . . are far greater than in any other area," the report said.

The consequences for the Arctic's environment would be dire, it said, wiping out populations of walrus, seal and polar bear and destroying the isolated indigenous communities that depend on hunting to survive.

Left undetected, a pipeline leak could spread oil beneath the surface of sea ice. Ice floes could carry oil hundreds of miles away from the source.

Getting to the scene of a spill would be a challenge. The nearest major port, Dutch Harbor, is 1,300 nautical miles away from the drilling areas in the Chukchi and Beaufort seas, and what few air landing strips exist are not connected to any road system. There are no coast guard vessels in either sea, and the nearest coast guard station is 950 miles by air away in Kodiak Alaska.

Response teams would confront gale-force winds, massive blocks of ice and turbulent seas, total darkness for six weeks of the year, and extreme cold. Cranes would freeze and chemical dispersants, such as those used to break up the BP spill, might not work.

Ice Could Help Spills Spread

Then there is the ice. Left undetected, a pipeline leak could spread oil beneath the surface of sea ice. Ice floes could carry oil hundreds of miles away from the source. At freeze-up, oil can become trapped within ice within the space of four hours, remaining there until spring. If it becomes trapped within multi-year ice, oil could stay in the environment for years, or even a decade, the report said.

Pew and other environment groups this week ramped up their campaigns on offshore drilling, taking out full-page advertisements in gulf newspapers calling on the Senate to pass tougher offshore drilling regulations when it returns for its lame-duck session next week.

An oil spill bill passed in the House last summer [2010], but has stalled in the Senate amid strong objection from the oil industry to provisions that would lift the current $75m [million] cap on liability.

There is also increasing concern that the interior secretary, Ken Salazar, will lift the hold placed on Arctic drilling permits after the oil disaster in the gulf.

Report Recommends More Research

The report does not call for a complete ban on Arctic drilling, but it recommends far more extensive study of the potential environmental impacts of a spill before industry is allowed to go-ahead. "We need to take a surgical approach and see what areas should and should not be allowed," said Heiman.

The report also says that any spill response has to be tailored to the extreme Arctic conditions, and that oil companies be required to real-life test runs of their containment efforts.

"We can't be training them the moment the oil hits the water and the ground like we did in the Gulf," Heiman said. "There is much more work that needs to be done to protect the Arctic."

Oil Companies Have
Not Kept Up with the Latest
Cleanup Technologies

Chris Wickham

Chris Wickham is the European science correspondent for the Reuters news agency.

With oil becoming scarcer and more expensive, the economics of the industry may finally tip in favor of one of the most neglected areas of its business—the technology for cleaning up oil spills.

Despite efforts by scientists to find new and more effective ways to deal with spilt oil, there has been little fundamental change in the technology in the two decades since the 1989 *Exxon Valdez* disaster that spilled 750,000 barrels of oil into Prince William Sound in Alaska.

But as oil companies push into the environmentally pristine Arctic and deeper waters elsewhere, the pressure on them to demonstrate they can quickly mop up spilt oil will increase.

Big spills like BP PLC's 2010 disaster in the Gulf of Mexico usually trigger a flurry of research, much like the acceleration in weapons technology in wartime, but history shows that industry and government enthusiasm quickly fades.

That loss of momentum could prove expensive. BP has already spent $14 billion on clean-up operations, paid out over $8 billion in claims and is offering a further $7.8 billion in settlement to those affected by the disaster.

Oil-Eating Gel

A pair of materials researchers from Pennsylvania State University has come up with a novel gel that can absorb 40 times its own weight in oil and forms a soft solid that is strong enough to be scooped up and fed straight into a refinery to recover the oil.

The polymer developed by Mike Chung and Xuepei Yuan only interacted with oil in tests and the swelled gel contained no water, which solves the sticky problem of separating spilt crude from the water it pollutes.

Chung says existing absorbers like straw, and even corn cobs, can only hold about five times their own weight. They also pick up water along with the oil and become waste that has to be buried in special landfills or burned.

Rival teams have applied nanotechnology to the problem to produce ultra-lightweight sponges that are oleophilic and hydrophobic—they love oil but repel water.

The Penn State scientists estimate their polymer gel could be produced on a large scale for $2 a pound, which is enough to recover more than five gallons of spilled oil worth roughly $12 based on a barrel price of $80.

"Had this material been applied to the top of the leaking well head in the Gulf of Mexico during the 2010 spill, this . . . could have effectively transformed the gushing brown oil into a floating gel for easy collection and minimized the pollution consequences," the scientists said in their research paper on the new material.

Nanotech Sponges

Rival teams have applied nanotechnology to the problem to produce ultra-lightweight sponges that are oleophilic and hydrophobic—they love oil but repel water.

Daniel Hashim and colleagues at Rice University in Houston have found a way to turn carbon nanotubes—atom-thick sheets of carbon rolled into cylinders—into a sponge material that sucks up oil and can either be squeezed or burned to remove it. In either case the fire-resistant sponge can be re-used.

Hashim told Reuters he has some seed capital from companies and individual investors to develop the technology but there are plenty of hurdles ahead.

Aside from the need to develop a system to deploy the sponge material into an oil spill, "the most significant barrier is equipment cost associated with the scale-up process," he said.

If those hurdles can be overcome, the material could be useful in the Arctic because it retains its sponginess even in extreme cold.

Even celebrities are getting in on the act. In June [2012], a U.S. jury ruled in favor of actor Kevin Costner in a lawsuit in which fellow actor Stephen Baldwin accused him of cheating in a multimillion dollar deal to sell oil clean-up devices to BP after the Gulf of Mexico spill.

A Flash in the Pan

Some industry insiders are candid about the problem. Writing in the *Journal of Petroleum Technology* in September [2012], Michael Cortez, BP's manager of oil spill response technology, and his deputy Hunter Rowe warned the research push since the Gulf disaster could be short-lived.

The industry has ramped up funding to improve response technology after other major spills, they said.

"In all instances, however, after a few years of progress, conditions changed in the industry because of oil price volatility and other economic events, and spill response technology development and funding returned to previous levels."

More than twenty years after *Exxon Valdez*, when BP's Macondo well spewed out an estimated 5 million barrels into the sea, the flotilla attacking the slick was still using floating booms to contain it, specially adapted ships that pick it up by skimming the surface of the water, and controversial chemical dispersants.

There have been advances, not least in the gadgetry for tracking and imaging spills and deploying the ships. The booms are better designed, the skimmers are more efficient and the dispersants less toxic. Some in the industry think this is enough.

"We believe the current technology we have more than meets the need," said Simon Henry, finance director of Royal Dutch Shell, when asked by Reuters whether the company was increasing research spending as it pushes exploration into the Arctic.

Shell, which is Europe's top oil company, was forced to suspend the hunt for oil in the Chukchi Sea off Alaska this year [2012] after a giant metal box designed to help contain the oil in the event of a well blowout, was damaged during tests.

Scientists are busy coming up with answers but in the end it will be the will of the oil industry and pressure from governments that determine how far and how fast these new technologies are taken up.

"We put most of our effort into ensuring there isn't a spill in the first place," said Henry, adding that a series of barriers, including the blowout preventer that sits on the sea floor at the well-head, are there to guard against "a very, very unlikely event".

A Sense of Urgency

Cortez and Rowe from BP argue that exploration in harsher and more remote environments calls for more cutting-edge spill response technology.

"The key to closing technology gaps and enhancing current technologies is to prevent the sense of urgency from being diminished," they said in their journal article.

Scientists are busy coming up with answers but in the end it will be the will of the oil industry and pressure from governments that determine how far and how fast these new technologies are taken up.

As for the novel oil-absorbing gel, Mike Chung is still waiting for the industry to call.

"There is a lot of interest in Petrogel technology for oil spill cleanup and recovery, but not from major oil companies," he told Reuters.

CHAPTER 4

Does the Oil Industry Need More Oversight and Regulation?

Overview: New US Oil Boom Puts Shale Fracking in the Spotlight

Adam Hurlburt

Adam Hurlburt is a staff writer for the Black Hills Pioneer, *a locally owned and independent newspaper in South Dakota.*

If oil and gas development came to northwestern South Dakota, hydraulic fracturing or "fracking" would come as well. And there's some debate in the public sector on the environmental and human health impacts surrounding this process.

Fracking and horizontal drilling technologies are almost completely responsible for the recent oil boom in North Dakota. The petroleum hydrocarbons in the Williston Basin are largely trapped in porous shale rock formations. The most effective way to access these trapped hydrocarbons is through a combination of horizontal drilling and hydraulic fracturing.

First a well is drilled straight down to a certain depth—usually some two miles beneath the earth's surface. That well is then encased in cement all the way down to prevent both hydraulic fracturing chemicals and petroleum from finding its way into aquifers or groundwater formations at various depths on the drilling path. Once that concrete has dried and has been tested at extremely high pressures to make sure it will hold up to the high pressure injection of a mixture of water, sand and miscellaneous chemicals that takes place in the fracking process, another drill is sent down into the well, which drills down farther, beyond the cement casing, until it reaches the shale formations that are rich with trapped petroleum. This is where horizontal drilling comes in. Little by little that

Adam Hurlburt, "Shale Oil, Fracking and Environmental Issues," *Black Hills Pioneer*, May 11, 2012. Reprinted by permission of the Black Hills Pioneer © 2013.

drill turns from vertical to horizontal, often drilling out two miles horizontally into the formation from the initial curve point. This is when hydraulic fracturing takes place. Some 10 million gallons of water, sand and miscellaneous hydraulic fracturing chemicals are pumped down into the well at immense pressure. This pressure builds up in the shale rock formations until it creates fissures in the rock, and through those fissures flows the oil and natural gas that have been trapped in the rock for millions of years. That's how it's been done in North Dakota and that's more than likely how it would be done in northwestern South Dakota.

Myriad Environmental Concerns

So what are the environmental and human health concerns behind this practice? There are a myriad. And officially, as far the Environmental Protection Agency is concerned, the jury is still out on the process. They're currently working on a study that they expect to release sometime in 2015. The concerns largely have to do with the contamination of groundwater/drinking water by fracking chemicals and natural gasses like methane, and to some extent the creation of manmade earthquakes via another part of the fracking process.

Australia has been so concerned by hydraulic fracturing and its related processes that it suspended the practice entirely nationwide from January to April of this year [2012]. Last year in the U.K., studies by the British Geological Survey concluded that two earthquakes were linked to nearby fracking operations. Ohio regulators recently determined that a rash of minor earthquakes in the state last year were very likely caused by the high pressure injection of hydraulic fracturing waste water into deep disposal wells. A recent study by the Colorado School of Public Health concluded that those living within a half mile of hydraulic fracturing operations faced higher risks of cancer.

A Geologist's Perspective

This is some scary stuff. But how scared should we be? Thankfully a panel of several official speakers at the Black Hills Bakken Oil Conference addressed these issues and more at the close of the second and final day of the conference, held last week [May 2012] in Spearfish. South Dakota State Geologist Derric Iles took on these environmental questions first.

"To be brutally factual, every time you frac a well you're causing an earthquake. It's the microcracks that you're developing under the ground; you can measure them with sensitive seismic instrumentation," Iles said. "We're concerned with the inducement of earthquakes that may cause physical damage on the surface, you know, the collapse of buildings, disruption of utilities or those sorts of things. I am not aware, in the U.S. anyhow, where the hydraulic fracturing process—not underground injection of waste, that's a separate issue—but the hydraulic fracturing process that has caused an earthquake of the kind that humans usually get upset about."

Iles stated that the confusion sets in when attempting to differentiate fracking itself and the high-pressure, deep underground injection of wastewater.

The oil industry can do wonderful things, but it cannot cause fractures two miles high through the earth's surface to get to useable aquifers.

Fracking vs. Wastewater Injection

"You've got a pipe in the ground, you're pumping something into it, it must be fracking. There is underground injection of waste," Iles said. "One of the examples that comes to my mind is a long time ago in Colorado at the Rocky Mountain Arsenal where they were, over a long period of time, under extremely high pressure, injecting waste under ground—which is a permitted, legal way to dispose of whatever it is you have. But what they had the unfortunate event to happen is that they activated an old fault. Essentially they greased the skids by the continual application of high pressure with the injection of fluid along an old fault line that they didn't know was there. When they stopped the injection, bingo, the earthquake stopped.

"There is a difference between long-term, high-pressure injection of underground waste and the instantaneous, relatively speaking, hydraulic fracturing of a well," Iles continued. "So, that's the earthquake side."

Iles then addressed the chemical/groundwater contamination side of the question, stating that in North Dakota, for example, they're fracking roughly two miles below the earth's surface.

Deep Fracking Protects Water

"That is far, far, far, below any drinking water source that we may access as humans," he said. "The oil industry can do wonderful things, but it cannot cause fractures two miles high through the earth's surface to get to useable aquifers.

"So the fear that we all read that says, 'oh my God, hydraulic fracturing is causing contamination of shallow ground water,' I personally am not aware of any case for hydraulic fracturing, the process of the hydraulic fracturing at depth has caused the contamination of shallow ground water," Iles continued. "Now, do humans do stupid things? You bet. Do we spill things on the land surface? Do we have accidents at land surface that caused the contamination of shallow ground water? Absolutely. Those are the things that happen. I don't think there's any documented case were the hydraulic fracturing at depth has caused shallow ground water contamination."

Buzz Skretteberg, a retired geologist for Superior and Exxon oil companies and Spearfish native with decades of experience in the oil industry, added to Iles' statement and said that there has been contamination from hydraulic fracturing in surface waters, but only if the fracturing was done very close to the level of those surface waters. He added that he too was unfamiliar with any cases of water contamination from fracking at depth.

"The last thing we want to do is ruin the drinking water sources that we have around the Black Hills, or in northwestern South Dakota, wherever it might be," Iles added. "I can assure that I personally am passionate not only about the potential for economic development in South Dakota, but I am equally passionate about protecting those resources for future generations and, I'm just not going to look the other way."

Following Best Practices

Lance Astrella, attorney at Denver's Astrella Law, P.C., has had decades of legal experience with the oil and gas industry and spends most of his time advising and representing individual land and mineral owners. He also weighed in on these environmental issues.

> *Requiring those best management practices, at this stage, is mostly the responsibility of individual land and mineral owners as well as local communities.*

Astrella stated that he agreed with everything that had been said about deep level fracking being safe as long as the companies responsible for the fracking are working within the guidelines of best management practices that work to minimize or eliminate altogether any unsavory side effects.

"The handling of flow-back fluid, storm water runoff, and seepage, if they're not handled correctly, can cause water contamination," Astrella said. "And then there is the migration up the back of the pipe of old wells. And there have been instances where there has been contamination through that. Of course, you can do what they call mechanical integrity tests on the old vertical wells to be sure that cement job stood strong before you do your horizontal frac. So it's one of those best management practices that ought to be followed to be sure there's not a pathway up into the aquifer.

"Going back to earthquakes," he continued. "Those earthquakes had to do with injection of class 2 disposal wells, disposal wells that take wastewater and fluids. It could be frac fluids that are being disposed of because they're not recycling and large volumes of waste product have to be disposed of. Secondly, you have a lot of water that's being injected that has nothing to do with fracs, it's produced water. In a lot of fields there's more water produced than oil and gas, and you have to inject those, that's why. And there's a pretty good body of evidence that it causes earthquakes. It happened in Oklahoma, it happened in Dallas, it happened in Arkansas, it happened more recently in Ohio. Again, best management practices. If it's produced water it should be cleaned up and processed. And that's the interface that regulators have to look at, to protect the water, to preserve the water while accommodating oil and gas development."

Regulation Is in Its Infancy

The general consensus of those on the panel was that horizontal drilling, hydraulic fracturing and they're related processes can be relatively harmless, at the extraction level, if best management practices are utilized each and every time. But with state and national level regulations on the process still in relative infancy, those best management practices may not always be practiced. Astrella pushed that requiring those best management practices, at this stage, is mostly the responsibility of individual land and mineral owners as well as local communities.

And while the [Barack] Obama administration recently released a new set of regulations that requires oil and gas companies drilling on public and Native American lands to publicly disclose the chemicals used in fracking operations, as well as set standards for the proper construction of wells and waste-water disposal operations, these regulations do not put a check on operations on private lands, where most of the shale oil drilling and exploration is taking place.

Astrella is right, individual land and mineral owners as well as local communities must be in the know about best management practices if they want to ensure safe, responsible drilling.

Offshore Drilling Still Urgently Needs Reform

Center for Biological Diversity

The Center for Biological Diversity is an Arizona-based nonprofit that works to protect endangered species and their ecosystems through legal action and scientific petitions.

A year after the explosion at the *Deepwater Horizon* rig and the oil spill that leaked more than 200 million gallons of oil and other toxic pollutants into the Gulf of Mexico, significant regulatory and policy problems with offshore drilling and production remain unaddressed. The Center for Biological Diversity has identified 10 key reforms needed to protect people, the environment and wildlife from offshore drilling in the Gulf, the Arctic and beyond.

1. **Close the Loophole**: Nearly all drilling projects in the Gulf of Mexico, including the Macondo well, received waivers—called "categorical exclusions"—exempting them from in-depth environmental review. In May 2010, President [Barack] Obama said the government would close the loophole; that has not occurred. While deepwater projects are now given an abbreviated environmental review, the categorical exclusion is still on the books. Drilling projects can be, and are still being, approved without environmental review. For the vast majority of drilling, which is in shallow water, the Bureau of Ocean Energy Management and Enforcement (formerly the Minerals Management Service) continues to invoke categorical exclusions. Also, in a flurry to get

deepwater rigs drilling again in 2011, the Obama administration explicitly stated that projects approved prior to the BP oil spill would not need new environmental analyses. The Obama administration must eliminate the "categorical exclusion" for drilling plans and permits, and it must require regulators to commit to a full, public and expert environmental review.

2. **Recognize Oil-spill Threats**: The Bureau continues to permit drilling based on flawed assumptions about the risks of drilling to the Gulf of Mexico's marine and coastal environment. Everyone was unprepared for the *Deepwater Horizon* oil spill in part because it was assumed that at most 30,000 barrels of oil might spill over the entire lifetime of drilling leases in the Gulf and that the most likely size of a large spill was 4,600 barrels. In just one day the *Deepwater Horizon* spill eclipsed these numbers, then continued to gush for months. In 2007, the government concluded that any deepwater spills would weather and degrade before reaching shore, and thus would have a minimal impact on the environment and wildlife. Now the Bureau has conceded that catastrophic oil spills are possible in light of *Deepwater Horizon*. Yet it is still discounting the risks of a spill while permitting dozens of new wells in both deep and shallow water. The Bureau must eradicate outdated assumptions that oil spills are unlikely and will have negligible impacts on the environment.

3. **Update Environmental Analyses**: Like oil-spill risks, past assumptions about environmental conditions in the Gulf need revising due to the oil-spill disaster. Hundreds of miles of coastline were oiled, and numerous dolphins, sea turtles and seabirds perished in the wake of the blowout. Most of the damage has yet to be discovered. The Gulf of Mexico is a biologically rich marine habitat,

but it is also a vulnerable ecosystem with endangered sea turtles, whales and other imperiled wildlife. Secretary Ken Salazar's Department of the Interior continues to approve drilling based on environmental conditions of the Gulf of Mexico *before* the oil spill, despite having admitted that its environmental analysis needs to be supplemented. The Bureau must revise its environmental impact statement for offshore oil and gas activities in the Gulf in light of the damage caused by the *Deepwater Horizon* explosion and spill, and it should take this into account prior to permitting new projects.

4. **Curb Expansion of Risky Drilling**: There are nearly 4,000 offshore oil and gas operations in the Gulf already, and the Obama administration is seeking to expand. Just before the *Deepwater Horizon* blowout, Interior Secretary Salazar announced plans for the largest U.S. expansion of offshore drilling in three decades. In the wake of the disaster, some of those areas are temporarily off the table, but others are still slated for new leases and development. Meanwhile, a recent report by the Interior Department revealed that more than two-thirds of offshore leases already issued in the Gulf of Mexico are inactive, without any oil exploration or production. Offshore drilling leases are a privilege and turn public resources into private benefit, so until and unless drilling is made completely safe new leases should be off the table.

5. **Stop the Noise**: Oil and gas exploration is an acoustic nightmare for marine mammals in the Gulf of Mexico, and the government has never complied with the laws intended to protect these animals from harassment and harm. Each year the Bureau hands out permits to oil companies to conduct seismic surveys to search for sub-sea reservoirs of oil and gas. These surveys are almost as

loud as explosives, and the noise can cause hearing loss, interfere with communications, and disrupt normal breeding and feeding of sperm whales and other marine mammals. All of these permits are in plain violation of the Marine Mammal Protection Act and Endangered Species Act. The Bureau needs to fully comply with environmental laws prior to approving noisy seismic survey activities, and should take steps to protect the most sensitive areas through closures.

6. **Reform the Oil-spill Liability Cap**: Under the current Oil Pollution Act, the industry avoids full liability and compensation for damages in three ways. First, liability for damages not caused by "gross negligence, willful misconduct or violation of applicable federal regulation" is capped at $75 million per incident. Second, the highest level of financial responsibility that an offshore drilling source must demonstrate is $150 million, even if the entity has engaged in a grossly negligent or unlawful way. Third, the oil-spill trust fund is vastly underfunded, presently containing approximately $2 billion. The solutions are straightforward: raise and/or eliminate the liability caps and ensure through a "pay in" or "insurance" system that all costs of spills such as the BP disaster are fully compensated. Congress needs to lift the liability cap and require that oil companies be held fully accountable for their drilling risks.

7. **Shore Up Safety Concerns**: Despite a new forensic report that the BP blowout preventer had a design defect, the Bureau has approved nearly a dozen new permits to drill in deepwater. The supposedly fail-safe blowout preventers are now known to be unable to cut through a bent pipe, and questions remain about whether they can cut through the thick joint sections that recur along the drill pipe. While the government has announced that it

will develop new safety standards, it has pushed through permits *before* instating new requirements that address blowout preventer failures. If blowout preventers are the last line of defense to prevent an oil spill, concerns about their performance should be addressed *prior* to signing off on new drilling.

8. **Review Use of Dangerous Dispersants:** Dispersants and dispersed oil have been shown to have significant negative impacts on many forms of marine life, including plankton, turtles, fish, corals and birds. Dispersants release toxic breakdown products from oil that, alone or in combination with oil droplets and dispersant chemicals, can make dispersed oil more harmful to marine life than untreated oil. Both the short-term and long-term impacts of dispersants on marine life have not been adequately tested. As acknowledged by the EPA, the long-term effects of dispersants on aquatic life are unknown. The dispersants used in response to the BP oil spill, Corexit 9500A and Corexit 9527A, are toxic chemicals with still-untold effects. They are suspected of contributing to giant underwater oil plumes that are moving through deep water and leaving a trail of damaged and dead sea life on the ocean floor. The Obama administration must ensure that if any dispersants are approved for oil-spill response, they undergo thorough scientific review and do not contribute to added harmful impacts on wildlife, including endangered species.

9. **Place a Permanent Moratorium on Arctic Drilling:** The sensitive and biologically rich Arctic is no place for offshore drilling. As we saw with the *Deepwater Horizon* oil spill, oil companies are unable to prevent or stop an oil spill that is gushing at tremendous pressure undersea. In the Arctic, whose remote, harsh and frozen waters make oil-spill response unavailable, a spill would

likely be impossible to stop. A ruptured well could be inaccessible for most of the year, oil-spill response equipment is distant, and dispersants may not work in cold water. And of course, the Arctic is a pristine and biologically rich ecosystem that is already under extreme stress from climate change. The Obama administration needs to call off plans for offshore drilling in the Arctic.

10. **Pursue Cleaner Energy**: Climate change is an over-arching threat to global biodiversity; we need to shift course to prevent its worst effects. If current carbon-pollution trends continue, scientists estimate that climate change will condemn one-third of the world's plants and animals to extinction by 2050 and threaten up to two-thirds with extinction by 2100. But we can save most of these plants and animals if we take decisive and rapid action to reduce greenhouse gas pollution. Rather than drilling risky offshore oil wells, the Obama administration must rigorously regulate greenhouse gases under the Clean Air Act and shift away from dirty energy.

Tar Sands Pipelines Are Not Sufficiently Regulated

Anthony Swift, Susan Casey-Lefkowitz, and Elizabeth Shope

Anthony Swift is an attorney with the Natural Resources Defense Council's (NRDC) International Program. Susan Casey-Lefkowitz is director of the program and leads the organization's campaign to stop dirty fuels and the expansion of tar sands and their pipelines. Elizabeth Shope is an NRDC advocate, working on the campaign against tar sands.

Tar sands crude oil pipeline companies may be putting America's public safety at risk as pipelines transporting tar sands crude oil into the United States are increasingly carrying a more abrasive and corrosive mix—diluted bitumen or "DilBit"—raising risks of spills and damage to communities along their paths. While the impacts of tar sands production are well known—destruction of Boreal forests and wetlands, high levels of greenhouse gas pollution, and immense amounts of toxic waste—less well known is the increased risk and potential harm that can be caused by transporting the raw form of tar sands oil (bitumen) through pipelines to refineries in the United States.

In the past, the vast majority of tar sands bitumen was upgraded in Canada before coming into the United States as synthetic crude oil. However, more often now bitumen is diluted and piped to U.S. refineries after being strip mined or melted from the tar sands under Canada's Boreal forest in Alberta. Bitumen is not the same as conventional oil; it has characteristics that make it potentially more dangerous. Nonetheless, the safety and spill response standards used by the

Anthony Swift, Susan Casey-Lefkowitz and Elizabeth Shope, "Tar Sands Safety Risks," nrdc.org, February 2011. Reprinted with permission from the Natural Resources Defense Council.

United States to regulate pipeline transport of bitumen are designed for conventional crude oil.

This report shows that with an increasing trend of more bitumen coming into U.S. pipelines, it is important that the American public understands the characteristics of bitumen in a pipe that are potentially a threat to health and safety. The United States needs to ensure that appropriate oil pipeline safety and spill response standards that address the higher risks associated with transporting corrosive and acidic bitumen are in place. Until these safety and spill response standards are adopted, the United States should put a hold on the consideration of new tar sands pipelines.

The Growth of DilBit

Tar sands crude oil pipeline companies are using conventional pipeline technology to transport diluted bitumen or "DilBit," a highly corrosive, acidic, and potentially unstable blend of thick raw bitumen and volatile natural gas liquid condensate. In order to become usable transportation fuels, DilBit can only be processed by certain refineries that have built the capacity to handle very heavy crudes. With Canadian upgraders operating at full capacity, oil companies have started transporting more of the raw tar sands to U.S. refineries that can either already take the heavier oil or need to build additional upgrading capacity.

As tar sands oil companies send increasing volumes of DilBit to the United States, the risks of pipeline spills are becoming more apparent.

Historically, the United States has imported the majority of tar sands crude from Canada in the form of synthetic crude oil, a substance similar to conventional crude oil that has already gone through an initial upgrading process. Importing tar sands oil into the United States as DilBit—instead of synthetic crude oil—is a recent and growing development. Without much public knowledge or a change in safety standards, U.S. pipelines are carrying increasing amounts of the corrosive raw form of tar sands oil. In fact, over the last ten years, Dil-Bit exports to the United States have increased almost fivefold, to 550,000 barrels per day (bpd) in 2010—more than half of the approximately 900,000 bpd of tar sands oil currently flowing into the United States. By 2019, Canadian tar sands producers plan to triple this amount to as much as 1.5 million bpd of DilBit.

DilBit is the primary product being transported through the new TransCanada Keystone pipeline that runs from Alberta's tar sands to Illinois and Oklahoma and also through Enbridge's recently-built Alberta Clipper pipeline, which terminates in Wisconsin. In addition, DilBit is transported through the existing Enbridge Lakehead system that brings both conventional oil and tar sands from the Canadian border to Minnesota, Wisconsin, Illinois, Indiana, and Michigan.

Transporting DilBit is also the primary purpose of TransCanada's proposed Keystone XL pipeline, which would run nearly 2000 miles from Alberta through some of America's most sensitive lands and aquifers on the way to refineries on the U.S. Gulf Coast. This infrastructure will lock the United States into a continued reliance on pipelines that may not be operated or regulated adequately to meet the unique safety requirements for DilBit for decades to come. As tar sands oil companies send increasing volumes of DilBit to the United States, the risks of pipeline spills are becoming more apparent. DilBit pipelines, which require higher operating temperatures and pressures to move the thick material through a pipe, appear to pose new and significant risks of pipeline leaks or ruptures due to corrosion, as well as problems with leak detection and safety problems from the instability of DilBit. For example, in July 2010, an Enbridge tar sands pipeline spilled over 840,000 gallons of diluted bitumen into Michigan's Kalamazoo River watershed.

DilBit Can Weaken Pipelines

There are many indications that DilBit is significantly more corrosive to pipeline systems than conventional crude. Bitumen blends are more acidic, thick, and sulfuric than conventional crude oil. DilBit contains fifteen to twenty times higher acid concentrations than conventional crudes and five to ten times as much sulfur as conventional crudes. It is up to seventy times more viscous than conventional crudes. The additional sulfur can lead to the weakening or embrittlement of pipelines. DilBit also has high concentrations of chloride salts which can lead to chloride stress corrosion in high temperature pipelines. Refiners have found tar sands derived crude to contain significantly higher quantities of abrasive quartz sand particles than conventional crude.

This combination of chemical corrosion and physical abrasion can dramatically increase the rate of pipeline deterioration. Despite these significant differences, PHMSA [the U.S. Department of Transportation Pipeline and Hazardous Materials Safety Administration] does not distinguish between conventional crude and DilBit when setting minimum standards for oil pipelines.

DilBit poses an elevated risk to the environment and public safety once a leak has occurred.

The risks of corrosion and the abrasive nature of DilBit are made worse by the relatively high heat and pressure at which these pipelines are operated in order to move the thick DilBit through the pipe. Industry defines a high pressure pipeline as one that operates over 600 pounds per square inch (psi). Due to the high viscosity or thickness of DilBit, pipelines—such as the Keystone tar sands pipeline—operate at pressures up to 1440 psi and at temperatures up to 158 degrees Fahrenheit. In contrast, conventional crude pipelines generally run at ambient temperatures and lower pressures.

Higher temperatures thin the DilBit and increase its speed through the pipeline. They also increase the speed at which acids and other chemicals corrode the pipeline. An accepted industry rule of thumb is that the rate of corrosion doubles with every 20 degree Fahrenheit increase in temperature. At high temperatures, the mixture of light, gaseous condensate, and thick, heavy bitumen, can become unstable. Variations in pipeline pressure can cause the natural gas liquid condensate to change from liquid to gas form. This creates gas bubbles within the pipeline. When these bubbles form and collapse they release bursts of high pressure that can deform pipeline metal. The instability of DilBit can render pipelines particularly susceptible to ruptures caused by pressure spikes.

Leaks in DilBit Pipelines Can Be Difficult to Detect

Leaks in DilBit pipelines are often difficult to detect. As stated above, as DilBit flows through a pipeline, pressure changes within the pipeline can cause the natural gas liquid condensate component to move from liquid to gas phase. This forms a gas bubble that can impede the flow of oil. Because this phenomenon—known as column separation—presents many of the same signs as a leak to pipeline operators, real leaks may go unnoticed. Because the proper response to column separation is to pump more oil through the pipeline, misdiagnoses can be devastating. During the Kalamazoo River spill, the Enbridge pipeline gushed for more than twelve hours before the pipeline was finally shut down, and initial investigation indicates that the pipeline's monitoring data were interpreted to indicate a column separation rather than a leak. Ultimately, emergency responders were not notified until more than nineteen hours after the spill began.

DilBit Is Risky to the Environment and Human Health

DilBit poses an elevated risk to the environment and public safety once a leak has occurred. While all crude oil spills are potentially hazardous, the low flash point and high vapor pressure of the natural gas liquid condensate used to dilute the DilBit increase the risk of the leaked material exploding. DilBit can form an ignitable and explosive mixture in the air at temperatures above 0 degrees Fahrenheit. This mixture can be ignited by heat, spark, static charge, or flame. In addition, one of the potential toxic products of a DilBit explosion is hydrogen sulfide, a gas which can cause suffocation in concentrations over 100 parts per million and is identified by producers as a potential hazard associated with a DilBit spill. Enbridge identified hydrogen sulfide as a potential risk to its field personnel during its cleanup of the Kalamazoo River spill.

DilBit contains benzene, polycyclic aromatic hydrocarbons, and n-hexane, toxins that can affect the human central nervous systems. A recent report filed by the Michigan Department of Community Health found that nearly 60 percent of individuals living in the vicinity of the Kalamazoo River spill experienced respiratory, gastrointestinal, and neurological symptoms consistent with acute exposure to benzene and other petroleum related chemicals. In addition to their short term effects, long term exposure to benzene and polycyclic aromatic hydrocarbons has been known to cause cancer.

DilBit also contains vanadium, nickel, arsenic, and other heavy metals in significantly larger quantities than occur in conventional crude. These heavy metals have a variety of toxic effects, are not biodegradable, and can accumulate in the environment to become health hazards to wildlife and people.

DilBit Spills Are Especially Hard to Clean Up

Clean up of DilBit poses special risks. The characteristics of DilBit create challenges for cleanup efforts in rivers and wetland environments. In the case of conventional oil spills, mechanical devices such as booms, skimmers, and sorbent materials—described by the Environmental Protection Agency

(EPA) as the primary line of defense against oil spills in the United States—contain and recover oil floating on the water surface. However, unlike conventional crude oils, the majority of DilBit is composed of raw bitumen which is heavier than water. Following a release, the heavier fractions of DilBit will sink into the water column and wetland sediments. In these cases, the cleanup of a DilBit spill may require significantly more dredging than a conventional oil spill. Further, heavy oil exposed to sunlight tends to form a dense, sticky substance that is difficult to remove from rock and sediments. Removing this tarry substance from river sediment and shores requires more aggressive cleanup operations than required by conventional oil spills. These factors increase both the economic and environmental costs of DilBit spills.

> *The majority of hazardous liquid pipelines in the United States are more than forty years old.*

The containment and cleanup of a DilBit spill requires significant personnel, equipment, supplies, and other resources. The Kalamazoo River spill required more than 2000 personnel, over 150,000 feet of boom, 175 heavy spill response trucks, 43 boats, and 48 oil skimmers. Federal regulations for crude oil pipeline spill response lack specific standards and mandatory equipment and personnel requirements, and are therefore much weaker than regulations for other polluters, such as oil tankers and oil refineries. While the Kalamazoo River spill occurred in a populated area where residents could notify authorities of the spill and significant private spill response equipment was nearby, other DilBit pipelines cross significantly more remote areas. In the entire area of Montana, Nebraska, North Dakota, and South Dakota, TransCanada—the operator of Keystone I and the proposed Keystone XL pipelines, and its private contractors—list a total of 8,000 feet of boom, eight spill response trailers, seven skimmers, and four boats available to respond to a spill. Much of this equipment will take hours to transport on-site in the event of a spill in this large region.

Pipeline Age Is a Factor

One indication of the potential additional hazards of DilBit to a pipeline is that the Alberta hazardous liquid pipeline system has a relatively high rate of pipeline failure from internal corrosion. While DilBit has not been common until recently in the United States pipeline system, it has composed a high proportion of the product on the Alberta pipeline system. In Alberta, tar sands producers have been using DilBit pipelines since the 1980s to move raw bitumen to upgrading facilities. By 2009, over two-thirds of all crude produced in Alberta was transported as DilBit at some point in its production process.

Over half of the pipelines currently operating in Alberta have been built in the last twenty years as the tar sands region developed. In contrast, the majority of hazardous liquid pipelines in the United States are more than forty years old. The older a pipeline is the more attention that a pipeline company needs to pay to it because it may not have the same type of coating, same strength of steel, or had corrosion protections for its entire life. Despite its relatively recent construction, Alberta's hazardous liquid system had 218 spills greater than 26 gallons per 10,000 miles of pipeline caused by internal corrosion from 2002 to 2010, compared to 13.6 spills greater than 26 gallons per 10,000 miles of pipeline from internal corrosion reported in the United States to PHMSA during that same time period. This rate of spills due to internal corrosion is sixteen times higher in Alberta than in the United States.

While differences in data collection and regulations between Alberta and the United States make it impossible to make a clear comparison of this data, the higher internal corrosion rates in Alberta certainly raise the yet unanswered question of whether the properties that are unique to DilBit are apt to cause the same corrosion problems in the United States as more and more DilBit flows south. . . .

Policy Recommendations

There are several steps that the United States can and should take in order to prevent future DilBit pipeline spills. These precautionary steps are essential for protecting farmland, wildlife habitat, and critical water resources—and should be put in place before rushing to approve risky infrastructure that Americans will be locked into using for decades to come.

> *Evaluate the need for new U.S. pipeline safety regulations.* Older safety standards designed for conventional oil may not provide adequate protection for communities and ecosystems in the vicinity of a DilBit pipeline. The Department of Transportation should analyze and address the potential risks associated with the transport of DilBit at the high temperatures and pressures at which those pipelines operate and put new regulations in place as necessary to address these risks.

> *The oil pipeline industry should take special precautions for pipelines transporting DilBit.* Until appropriate regulations are in place, oil pipeline companies should use the appropriate technology to protect against corrosion of their pipelines, to ensure that the smallest leaks can be detected in the shortest time that is technologically possible, and companies should ensure sufficient spill response assets are in place to contain a spill upon detection.

> *Improve spill response planning for DilBit pipelines.* Spill response planning for DilBit pipelines should be done through a public process in close consultation with local emergency response teams and communities.

> *New DilBit pipeline construction and development should not be considered until adequate safety regulations for DilBit pipelines are in place.* The next major proposed DilBit pipeline is

TransCanada's Keystone XL pipeline. This pipeline approval process should be put on hold until PHMSA evaluates the risks of DilBit pipelines and ensures that adequate safety regulations for DilBit pipelines are in place.

Reduce U.S. demand for oil, especially for tar sands oil. The United States can dramatically cut oil consumption by reinforcing existing reduction programs, such as efficiency standards for vehicles, and through new investments in alternatives to oil.

Congress Should Reform Oil Spill Liability Laws

Nicolas D. Loris, Jack Spencer, and James Jay Carafano

Nicolas D. Loris is a research fellow at the Thomas A. Roe Institute for Economic Policy Studies at The Heritage Foundation; Jack Spencer is a research fellow in nuclear energy at the Roe Institute. James Jay Carafano is deputy director of The Heritage Foundation's Davis Institute for International Studies; he is also director of the Allison Center for Foreign Policy Studies, a division of the Davis Institute.

Current law states that oil or gas companies do not have to pay more than $75 million in liability costs for accidents they cause—no matter how great the damages. Republicans and Democrats agree that the cap is too low. But simply raising it to another artificial level, or eliminating it entirely without other reforms, is not the easy answer, tempting as it might seem. A higher cap, or none at all, means very little as long as crucial safety, regulatory, and liability issues continue to be ignored, and public concerns are unaddressed. Government regulatory oversight is necessary, but liability insurance must be privately managed, with claims assessed and paid out by an independent administrator. Safety and preparedness measures must also be independently reviewed and approved. Above all, taxpayers must be protected from footing the liability costs for industry-caused disasters. The Heritage Foundation provides a comprehensive plan for responsible and commonsense measures to ensure offshore oil and gas safety, keeping the public informed and government bureaucracy in check. . . .

The Liability Cap Issue

The *Deepwater Horizon* oil spill in the Gulf of Mexico has brought a number of important policy issues regarding offshore drilling to the surface. One contentious issue is the extent to which offshore oil and gas operators are held liable for any accidents they may cause. Republicans and Democrats agree that the current liability cap of $75 million is too low. Members of Congress have called to raise the cap to $10 billion or remove it entirely.

The problem with these approaches is that they do not address the fundamental problem of the current system: It does not sufficiently align risk and liability with individual behavior. It starts with a very low liability cap and then forces all participants to contribute to a government-mandated trust fund to pay for damages. The result is a system that socializes risk by spreading the costs across the entire industry, creating a divide between behavior and financial risk. Simply raising the cap without more comprehensive reform would fail to fix the systemic problems and could effectively shut down offshore drilling entirely if activities are made unreasonably and artificially burdensome.

A Three-Point Plan

Instead of simply increasing or removing the cap, Congress and the Administration should develop a new approach that accurately assigns risk to all offshore operations, including exploratory drilling, production, and tanker movements; holds operators fully liable for their actions; and guards against frivolous lawsuits. Such a system should rely on market-based mechanisms and be built around private insurers and professional risk assessors.

Specifically, such a regime should include:

1. A multi-tiered insurance and liability system that relies on private insurance to cover liability for normal operations and a voluntary insurance pool for liability exceeding $1 billion;

2. An industry-funded organization governed by an inpendent board to reduce the likelihood of spills by setting and enforcing safety standards at individual sites, collecting safety data, sharing best practices, and working with government regulators; and

3. A pre-positioned industry-funded preparedness and response capability, certified by an independent organization, to deal aggressively and effectively with accidents if they do happen, as well as a more robust and integrated federal oversight and national response.

Congress should reform the Oil Spill Liability Trust Fund and remove the $75 million liability cap, replacing it with a new system that accurately assesses the risks of offshore oil and gas operations and appropriately assigns those risks to industry operators.

All three pieces—insurance, safety standards and inspection, and preparedness and response will work together to reduce the likelihood that a future spill will occur, and reduce the economic and environmental damage if it does occur.

Current Law

Oil spill costs should be regarded as consisting of two basic types: cleanup costs and liability costs. First, under current law, the responsible party must pay all cleanup costs. This approach is correct and needs no reform. Second, the liability costs are the costs incurred by individuals, businesses, and communities that suffer as a result of the oil spill. Under U.S. law for offshore facilities, the responsible party (in the *Deepwater Horizon* case, BP) is directly responsible for no more than $75 million of these costs. Liability costs above $75 million up to $1 billion are funded by the Oil Spill Liability Trust Fund (OSLTF). The OSLTF is financed by an eight-cent-per-barrel tax on imported and domestic oil.

The $75 million cap is waived if the responsible party is found to have acted with gross negligence or willful misconduct, an issue which has not yet been resolved regarding BP. Even so, BP has repeatedly stated it will pay all costs incurred by the oil spill. Although the current system seems to be working in terms of BP financing the full costs of its mistakes, the problem is how it impacts normal operations and procedures elsewhere in the industry. The Oil Pollution Act of 1990 addresses liability for onshore and offshore oil and gas operations. While this paper focuses only on offshore operations, its principles and concepts could apply to the oil and gas industry broadly.

A New, Market-Based Approach

Congress should reform the Oil Spill Liability Trust Fund and remove the $75 million liability cap, replacing it with a new system that accurately assesses the risks of offshore oil and gas operations and appropriately assigns those risks to industry operators. Companies must demonstrate to federal regulators an ability to insure against the liability risk associated with specific offshore oil and gas operations (exploration, extraction, and transportation, etc.) in federal waters. Private risk assessors will determine liability-coverage requirements for specific activities and federal regulators will certify that liability requirements are met. The means for meeting liability-coverage requirements will not be limited, but may include self-insurance, insurance pools, dedicated assets, or private insurance policies. The federal government will create a private, tiered insurance framework and administrative process to manage claims. The central element of the insurance framework will be a private and voluntary pooled insurance fund for claims above $1 billion. The claims process will ensure that legitimate claims are paid fully and efficiently while protecting responsible parties from frivolous lawsuits. . . .

Thoughtful Reform Is Needed

By simply raising or eliminating the liability cap, Congress is trying to solve a puzzle without all the pieces. Instead of reactively creating another arbitrary cap, Congress should wait to see how much the Gulf oil spill is likely to cost and allow private insurers to assess the true risk of offshore oil and gas operations.

Congress should create a liability system that clearly identifies risks and allocates associated liabilities, ensures that those engaged in the industry can meet their potential liabilities, protects industry from frivolous lawsuits, and assures the public that both environmental and economic damages from an oil spill can be addressed in full. The oil industry should create an independent safety organization that would provide an incentive for oil companies to explore and implement new safety and prevention mechanisms. While such an organization would greatly reduce the likelihood of spills in the future, the industry also needs to demonstrate a clear and full ability to respond competently in the event of a spill. These reforms would keep oil and gas operation safe, the public informed, and overzealous regulators in check.

Oil Industry Regulation Hurts the American Economy

K.J. Webb

K.J. Webb is editor-at-large for the Greater Tulsa Reporter, *a daily newspaper in Oklahoma, the largest oil producing state in the country.*

On a daily basis Americans reap the benefits of our nation's energy industry by flying, driving, using natural gas for a wide variety of important purposes, and using any of the 6,000 products of which petroleum is a fundamental component. Most do not think about how integral the domestic energy industry is to their daily lives. If so, they would be concerned about the continuing drilling moratoriums and trend towards heavy federal regulation that has been creeping over the energy industry for the past three years. It is essential to understand what's going on at the national policy level, which directly impacts . . . independent producers, jobs and the economy.

Limits imposed on domestic energy exploration have been a key issue impacting the energy industry, the economy and American jobs. The ongoing moratorium on drilling in the 19-million acre Arctic National Wildlife Refuge (ANWR) has been a contentious issue for years. According to the Department of the Interior's 1987 resource evaluation report of ANWR's Coastal Plain, there is an estimated 4.8–9.2 billion barrels of recoverable oil, which would go a long way in helping America achieve energy independence. Arguing for drilling in ANWR, energy industry experts cite new and proven drilling technologies that impose minimal environmental impact, hundreds of thousands of new jobs, and over $100 billion in potential tax and royalty revenue for the government. Despite the benefits of opening ANWR for exploration, and the majority of Alaskans supporting opening ANWR for exploration, the moratorium remains in place.

By proposing to end tax cuts for the energy industry, the government is further crippling the nation's energy industry and the economy.

Untapped Potential

ANWR isn't the only area that could provide the nation with tremendous and much-needed natural energy resources. According to a recent study by the largest economics consulting firm in Alaska, Northern Economics, with the University of Alaska Anchorage's Institute of Social and Economic Research, there is tremendous energy potential in the Alaska Arctic outer continental shelf (OCS) development in the Chukchi and Beaufort Seas. According to the report, the Arctic OCS development would generate nearly 10 billion barrels of oil and 15 trillion cubic feet of natural gas. Moreover, exploration and production would create an estimated 54,700 new jobs, generate a $145 billion payroll, and generate $193 billion in federal, state and local government revenue. The American Petroleum Institute (API) has recently called on the [Barack] Obama administration to open up Alaska's OCS region for exploration and production and adopt an energy policy that boosts rather than inhibits the nation's economy. Important to note is that there are other areas in the country with an abundance of oil. The U.S. Geological Survey reported in 2008 that the Bakken Formation, stretching from Northern Montana into North Dakota, holds 3 to 4.3 billion barrels of recoverable oil, 1.85 trillion cubic feet of associated/dissolved natural gas, and 148 million barrels of natural gas liquids.

Federal Agencies Hamper Progress

However, the Environmental Protection Agency (EPA) is threatening the energy industry's ability to recover the Bakken oil. This is because hydraulic fracturing (pumping a water-sand mixture into underground rock layers where the oil or gas is trapped) is required. Despite the EPA admitting that it knows of no case of hydraulic fracturing ever contaminating water supplies, and studies by the U.S. EPA and the Ground Water Protection Council have confirmed no direct link between hydraulic fracturing operations and groundwater impacts, the EPA continues to pursue regulations that burden the energy industry.

The Permian Basin, a major oil producing region in West Texas and Southeast New Mexico is under threat from the U.S. Fish and Wildlife Service. The Service has proposed to list a three-inch Dune Sagebrush lizard to the Endangered Species List, arguing that the lizard's habitat is fragmented by the oil and gas, wind turbine, and agriculture industries. A decision about adding the lizard to the list is expected by mid-December [2012]. If added to the list, it would devastate the towns in the Permian Basin, where 70 percent of the economy, and the majority of jobs, depend on the oil and gas industry.

In addition to increasing regulatory burdens on exploration, by proposing to end tax cuts for the energy industry, the government is further crippling the nation's energy industry and the economy. A July 2011 study sponsored by the American Energy Alliance (AEA) confirms that current proposals to carve out U.S. energy firms from receiving certain tax deductions would have a net negative impact on federal revenues. The study, by Louisiana State University Endowed Chair of Banking and nationally-renowned economist Dr. Joseph Mason, found that eliminating the energy industry's tax deductions will result in: $30 billion in federal tax revenue at the expense of $341 billion in economic output; a loss of 155,000 jobs; $68 billion in lost wages, and $83.5 billion in reduced tax revenues. Mason points out the extremely large role that the energy industry plays in the country's economy, contributing more than $1 trillion in 2008 alone.

Industry Tax Breaks Help Economy

According to Mason, eliminating the tax deductions on the U.S. oil and gas companies is grossly counterproductive to increasing federal revenues. Actually, the net impact on federal revenues of eliminating these tax deductions would be negative, resulting in adding hundreds of billions to the to the current $1.4 trillion U.S. deficit and $14.8 trillion U.S. debt.

Clearly, there is much at stake for the economy and jobs, particularly so for Oklahomans where the energy industry is a backbone of the state's economy, a major economic driver and jobs provider. It's time for Oklahomans to join to the conversation about national energy policy. Even though D.C. is miles away, energy policy decisions made in the Capitol will have a tremendously heavy impact on the lives of people in this state.

More Regulation
Is Not the Answer to
Oil Production Risks

Gerald P. O'Driscoll Jr.

Gerald P. O'Driscoll Jr. is a senior fellow at the Cato Institute, a libertarian think tank. He was formerly vice president at the Federal Reserve Bank of Dallas and later a vice president at Citigroup.

The Gulf oil spill and the global financial crisis both demonstrate the failings of big government. Partisan politics obscures the linkage, with the consequence that each political party repeats the mistakes of the other as its turn to govern arrives.

First, consider the oil spill. BP and its contractors are surely responsible for the accident. They may also be responsible for a poor response. The nature and scope of legal culpability is yet to be determined. What is the government's role? Offshore drilling is a dangerous activity with potential undesirable consequences now actualized. For this reason, as we have learned, it is heavily regulated. The agency directly responsible for regulating the activity is the Minerals Management Service (MMS) of the Department of the Interior.

Government regulation is intended to protect the public interest against bad or irresponsible behavior by private parties. In the case of offshore drilling, the federal government has assumed the role of solving a collective action problem. Potentially all Americans benefit from the drilling, but those living in coastal areas suffer disproportionate harm from mishaps. The government theoretically negotiates on their behalf and establishes rules to protect them.

"Regulatory Capture" Defined

Obviously, regulation failed. By all accounts, MMS operated as a rubber stamp for BP. It is a striking example of regulatory capture: Agencies tasked with protecting the public interest come to identify with the regulated industry and protect its interests against that of the public. The result: Government fails to protect the public. That conclusion is precisely the same for the financial services industry.

Financial services have long been subject to detailed regulation by multiple agencies. In his book on the financial crisis, *Jimmy Stewart is Dead*, Boston University Professor Laurence Kotlikoff counts over 115 regulatory agencies for financial services. If more hands in the pot helped, financial services would be in fine shape. Few believe such is the case.

Advocates of heavy regulation promise that risky behavior by banks can be controlled and limited by regulators. There are two major reasons such efforts fail. I have already discussed the first: regulatory capture.

In reaching to do more, big government accomplishes less. That is not an ideological statement, but an empirical observation.

The second source of regulatory failure is the knowledge problem identified by Nobel Laureate Friedrich Hayek. The knowledge required by regulators is dispersed throughout the industry and broader economy. For regulation to work, that dispersed knowledge must be centralized in the regulatory agency. To successfully accomplish this requires central planning of the industry, if not the economy. But the local knowledge of specific circumstances of time and place cannot be aggregated in one mind or agency. We know that is impossible, and that impossibility was the reason for the collapse of the Soviet Empire and the transformation of the Chinese economy.

From Market Economy to Crony Capitalism

Regulatory practice represents islands of central planning in otherwise decentralized market economies. If we add back in the problem of regulatory capture, then we get industries coddled and protected by government. When business and politics become intertwined we move from market economies to crony capitalism.

What is the missed lesson from all this? When President George W. Bush had his Katrina moment, the federal government's bumbling response was blamed on him, on the Republicans, and on conservatives. Now it is President [Barack] Obama's turn. His administration's faltering response to the disaster in the Gulf is attributed to his personal failings, staff ineptitude, communication failures, etc. And, of course, the two administrations have shared responsibility for the poor handling of the financial crisis.

A big-government conservative administration failed in crisis, as has a big-government liberal administration. The regulatory state did not prevent excessive risk taking whether in financial services, nor perhaps in offshore oil drilling. Government response to crises once they occur is slow and inept. All this is not because either Republicans or Democrats are in power, but because big government doesn't work. It can't deliver on its promises. Big government overpromises and underdelivers. In reaching to do more, big government accomplishes less. That is not an ideological statement, but an empirical observation.

History Repeats Itself

In the case of financial services, virtually all the proposed regulatory reform offers more of the same. Additional regulations will be added to existing ones without addressing why existing ones failed to prevent the crisis. The same process will likely happen with respect to offshore drilling.

[Albert] Einstein famously defined insanity as the belief that, if we repeatedly do the same thing, we will eventually get a different result. The response to the financial crisis, as to others, is policy insanity.

University of Chicago law professor Richard Epstein has observed that we need simple rules for a complex world. The complexity of rules is self-defeating, because that complexity requires more knowledge than can be acquired. Brazil has a simple rule for directors of failed banks: They are personally liable. That concentrates the mind of directors on reining in risk-taking by management more effectively than would creating a systemic-risk regulator.

The Obama administration and Congress propose more of the same failed approach to regulation. Instead they should heed Hayek, who observed that "the curious task of economics is to demonstrate to men how little they really know about what they imagine they can design."

Organizations to Contact

The editors have compiled the following list of organizations concerned with the issues debated in this book. The descriptions are derived from materials provided by the organizations. All have publications or information available for interested readers. The list was compiled on the date of publication of the present volume; the information provided here may change. Be aware that many organizations take several weeks or longer to respond to inquiries, so allow as much time as possible.

American Petroleum Institute (API)
1220 L St. NW, Washington, DC   20005-4070
(202) 682-8000
website: www.api.org

The American Petroleum Institute (API) is the national trade association for the oil and natural gas industry. API represents producers, refiners, suppliers, pipeline operators, and marine transporters, as well as the service and supply companies that support all segments of the industry. API speaks for the petroleum industry to the public, federal and state governments, and the media. The api.org website includes transcripts of congressional testimony on issues related to oil spills and their prevention and cleanup, as well as a variety of reports, including "Spill Response in the Arctic Offshore" and "Denying or Delaying Keystone XL Is Reckless Policy." The Institute also publishes the EnergyTomorrow.org website, which features extensive information about oil and natural gas exploration as well as a variety of news, blogs, and Twitter feeds.

British Petroleum (BP)
Warrenville Offices, Americas Business Service Center
Customer Service 28301 Ferry Rd., Warrenville, IL   60555
(800) 333-3991
e-mail: bpconsum@bp.com
website: www.bp.com

One of the largest international oil companies, British Petroleum (BP) is the company that owned the *Deepwater Horizon* well in the Gulf of Mexico when it failed in 2010. Information about BP's response to the Gulf oil spill can be found on the company's website, which includes an overview of the event, videos, pictures, maps, and additional information about the spill and the company's response. The site also features news updates about the still-evolving legal issues and court judgments related to the incident. BP is also involved in developing tar sands oil in Canada, and the BP website features a corporate presentation regarding that issue as well, titled "Canadian Oil Sands Slide Presentation."

Cato Institute
1000 Massachusetts Ave. NW, Washington, DC   20001-5403
(202) 842-0200 • fax: (202) 842-3490
website: www.cato.org

Cato Institute is a libertarian organization dedicated to the promotion of individual liberty, limited government, and free markets. As such, Cato scholars have called for drilling in the waters off the American coast to meet the ever-increasing US demand for oil. In response to the Gulf oil spill, Cato's fellows worried that the accident would do more to discourage continued exploration of offshore drilling options and result in increased regulatory measures that would do little to address the root problems that caused the spill to occur. Articles such as "Gulf Oil Spill: Same Old Arguments," "The Gulf Spill and Compensation for Disaster Victims," and "The Gulf Spill, the Financial Crisis, and Government Failure," all examine different aspects of the gulf spill and the government's response.

The Coastal Response Research Center (CRRC)
and Center for Spills in the Environment (CSE)
Gregg Hall, University of New Hampshire, 35 Colovos Rd.
Durham, NH   03824
(603) 862-1545 • fax: (603) 862-3957
e-mail: kathy.mandsager@unh.edu
website: www.crrc.unh.edu

The Coastal Response Research Center (CRRC) was established as a partnership between the National Oceanic and Atmospheric Administration (NOAA) and the University of New Hampshire (UNH) in 2004. The Center for Spills in the Environment (CSE) is a UNH center that expands the scope of interaction and cooperation with the private sector, other government agencies, and universities. The CRRC partnership stimulates innovation in spill preparedness, response, assessment, and implementation of spill recovery best practices. The CSE works to identify needs, evaluate, and demonstrate promising technologies and foster their use as part of new, integrative approaches to response and restoration. The organizations' joint website devotes special sections to the *Deepwater Horizon* blowout, Arctic response issues, and chemical dispersants, in addition to offering an extensive archive of news links and a bibliography of publications by center members and affiliates.

Counterspill

e-mail: info@counterspill.org
website: www.counterspill.org

Founded by documentary filmmaker Chris Paine in the wake of the Gulf oil disaster in 2010, Counterspill is an online project about nonrenewable energy disasters. The organization's mission is to counteract the ability of the energy industry to control the public narrative about oil spills and other energy disasters through their corporate propaganda. The Counterspill website offers a wide variety of news articles, videos, and interactive tools for learning about oil spills and other energy disasters around the world. The site features an extensive archive of background articles about both historical spills and current events, and site visitors can sign up for the Counterspill e-mail newsletter and Twitter or RSS feeds.

Greenpeace, USA

702 H St. NW, Suite 300, Washington, DC   20001
(202) 462-1177 • fax: (202) 462-4507

e-mail: info@wdc.greenpeace.org
website: www.greenpeace.org

Greenpeace is an environmental organization dedicated to protecting the global environment through the use of confrontational but peaceful means that directly engage those involved in actions seen as destructive by the organization. These campaigns are undertaken in an attempt to raise awareness about environmental threats worldwide. Following the Gulf oil spill, Greenpeace published information chronicling the event on its website with a timeline, videos, and images of the destruction, as well as information about how the next disaster could be averted.

The Heritage Foundation
214 Massachusetts Ave. NE, Washington, DC   20002-4999
(202) 546-4400
website: www.heritage.org

The Heritage Foundation is a conservative think tank that seeks to create and advocate for public policies that espouse the ideals of free enterprise, limited government, individual freedom, traditional American values, and a strong national defense. The organization has promoted the benefits of offshore drilling for the American people, the environment, and the economy. Following the Gulf oil spill, Heritage published a report titled "Stopping the Slick, Saving the Environment: A Framework for Response, Recovery, and Resiliency," which criticized the federal government's response to that point and encouraged them to take a more proactive approach to limiting the damage to the environment, wildlife, economy, and culture on the US Gulf coast. This report and additional information about the spill can be found on the organization's website.

International Tanker Owners Pollution Federation (ITOPF)
1 Oliver's Yard, 55 City Rd., London   EC1Y 1HQ
   United Kingdom
+44 20 7566 6999 • fax: +44 20 7566 6950

e-mail: central@itopf.com
website: www.itopf.com

The International Tanker Owners Pollution Federation (ITOPF) is a nonprofit organization established on behalf of the world's shipowners and their insurers to promote effective response to marine spills of oil, chemicals, and other hazardous substances. Technical services include emergency response, advice on cleanup techniques, pollution damage assessment, assistance with spill response planning, and the provision of training. ITOPF is a source of comprehensive information on marine oil pollution.

The National Commission on the Deepwater Horizon Oil Spill and Offshore Drilling
website: www.oilspillcommission.gov

President Barack Obama established The National Commission on the Deepwater Horizon Oil Spill and Offshore Drilling by executive order on May 21, 2010. Its purpose was to thoroughly examine the facts and circumstances concerning the causes of the *Deepwater Horizon* explosion and to develop options to prevent and mitigate any future offshore oil spills. The Commission ceased operations in March 2011, but its website will remain active in perpetuity. Background papers, Congressional hearing transcripts, correspondence, videos, and other materials produced by the Commission are available from the site, as is the Commission's final report, "Deep Water: The Gulf Oil Disaster and the Future of Offshore Drilling."

National Oceanic and Atmospheric Administration Office of Response and Restoration (OR&R)
1305 East-West Highway, Silver Spring, MD   20910
(301) 713-4248 • fax: (301) 713-4389
e-mail: orr.spills@noaa.gov
website: http://response.restoration.noaa.gov

The National Oceanic and Atmospheric Administration's Office of Response and Restoration (OR&R) prepares for, evaluates, and responds to threats to coastal environments, including oil spills. During a spill, OR&R provides scientific support to the US Coast Guard officers in charge of response operations. In addition to spill response software and mapping tools, OR&R provides standard techniques and publishes guidelines for observing oil, assessing shoreline impact, and evaluating accepted cleanup technologies. A section of the organization's website titled "Oil and Chemical Spills" features a variety of information pertaining specifically to oil spills, types of oil, drilling activities in the Arctic, and spill containment. There is also a section dedicated to the 2010 *Deepwater Horizon* incident that features extensive information about the incident and its cleanup and aftermath. Site visitors can also sign up for the OR&R's monthly e-newsletter.

Natural Resources Defense Council (NRDC)
40 West 20th St., New York, NY   10011
(212) 727-2700 • fax: (212) 727-1773
e-mail: nrdcinfo@nrdc.org
website: www.nrdc.org

The Natural Resources Defense Council (NRDC) promotes the international protection of wildlife and wild places through law, science, and a membership of over one million people. Some of the main focuses of the organization include climate change, alternative energy, and protection of the world's oceans and endangered habitats. The NRDC website offers in-depth information about the *Deepwater Horizon* spill, including an interactive map that allows visitors to "Go Below the Surface of the Gulf Oil Disaster." The NRDC strongly opposes development of the proposed Keystone XL Pipeline, which would carry heavy tar sands oil from Canada to refineries on the US Gulf coast. The organization's site features numerous fact sheets, news items, and reports concerning the Keystone XL issue, as well as opportunities for individuals to get involved with its campaign against its development.

Sierra Club
85 Second St., 2nd Floor, San Francisco, CA   94105
(415) 977-5500 • fax: (415) 977-5799
e-mail: information@sierraclub.org
website: www.sierraclub.org

One of the nation's oldest environmental organizations, the Sierra Club was founded in 1892 and has been working to protect and conserve the nation's environment ever since. In the wake of the Gulf oil spill, the Sierra Club advocated on behalf of the individuals living in the Gulf region and worked to ensure that the clean up of the oil minimized lasting damage to wildlife and ecosystems in the area. A variety of reports and multimedia concerning the spill can be accessed on the Sierra Club website. The Sierra Club strongly opposes development of the Keystone XL Pipeline, and a variety of materials concerning Keystone XL is available on the site as well.

US Environmental Protection Agency (EPA)
Ariel Rios Building, 1200 Pennsylvania Ave. NW
Washington, DC   20460
(202) 272-0167
website: www.epa.gov

The US Environmental Protection Agency (EPA) is the government agency designated to ensure that both human and environmental health in the United States are protected and preserved. With regional and specialized offices nationwide, the agency works to influence and promote positive environmental stewardship and policies. The EPA conducted numerous tests following the BP oil spill, monitored conditions, and assessed the dispersants used to try to help clean the waters where the spill occurred. Information about the results of these tests can be found on the EPA website.

US Fish and Wildlife Service (USFWS)
4401 N. Fairfax Dr., Suite 340, Arlington, VA   22203
(800) 344-WILD
website: www.fws.gov

The US Fish and Wildlife Service is a bureau within the US Department of the Interior that works to ensure that fish, animals, and plants in the United States are protected and conserved for future generations to enjoy. This bureau is in charge of implementing the Natural Resource Damage Assessment and Restoration Program in response to oil spills, including the *Deepwater Horizon* spill. Information about the USFWS's role in recent spills of national interest can be found on the bureau's website along with maps, videos, multimedia, news releases, interviews, and other information about oil spills and their cleanup. The page titled "Oil Spill Preparation and Response" is the place to find spill-related information on the site.

US Senate Committee on Energy and Natural Resources
304 Dirksen Senate Bldg., Washington, DC   20510
(202) 224-4971 • fax: (202) 224-6163
website: www.energy.senate.gov

The US Senate Committee on Energy and Natural Resources is the congressional body that has jurisdiction over matters related to energy and public lands. Its far-reaching legislative activity covers energy resources and development, regulation and conservation, strategic petroleum reserves, public lands and their renewable resources, surface mining, federal coal, oil and gas and other mineral leasing, and water resources. Transcripts for testimony related to oil exploration, spill prevention and response, and the Keystone XL Pipeline are archived on the Committee's website.

Bibliography

Books

Samuel Avery and Bill McKibben — *The Pipeline and the Paradigm: Keystone XL, Tar Sands, and the Battle to Defuse the Carbon Bomb.* Washington, DC: Ruka Press, 2013.

Sharon Bushell and Ellen Wheat — *The Spill: Personal Stories from the Exxon Valdez Disaster.* Seattle: Epicenter Press, 2009.

William Freudenburg and Robert Gramling — *Blowout in the Gulf: The BP Oil Spill Disaster and the Future of Energy in America.* Boston: MIT Press, 2012.

Antonia Juhasz — *Black Tide: The Devastating Impact of the Gulf Oil Spill.* Hoboken, NJ: John Wiley and Sons, 2011.

Ezra Levant — *Ethical Oil: The Case for Canada's Oil Sands.* Toronto: McClelland and Stewart, 2011.

Abrahm Lustgarten — *Run to Failure: BP and the Making of the Deepwater Horizon Disaster.* New York: W.W. Norton and Co., 2012.

Lisa Margonelli — *Oil on the Brain: Petroleum's Long, Strange Trip to Your Tank.* New York: Broadway, 2008.

Leonardo Maugeri — *The Age of Oil: What They Don't Want You to Know About the World's Most Controversial Resource.* Guilford, CT: The Lyons Press, 2007.

National Commission on the BP Deepwater Horizon Oil Spill and Offshore Drilling	*Deep Water: The Gulf Oil Disaster and the Future of Offshore Drilling.* Washington, DC: National Commission on the BP Deepwater Horizon Oil Spill and Offshore Drilling, 2011.
Andrew Nikiforuk	*Tar Sands: Dirty Oil and the Future of a Continent.* Vancouver: Greystone, 2010.
Nuka Research/Pearson Consulting	*Oil Spill Prevention and Response in the U.S. Arctic Ocean: Unexamined Risks, Unacceptable Consequences.* Washington, DC: Pew Environment Group, 2010.
Bob Reiss	*The Eskimo and the Oil Man: The Battle at the Top of the World for America's Future.* New York: Business Plus, 2012.
Merle Savage	*Silence in the Sound: Aftermath of Exxon Valdez Oil Spill.* Seattle: CreateSpace, 2010.
Sonia Shah	*Crude: The Story of Oil.* New York: Seven Stories Press, 2006.

Periodicals and Internet Sources

American Petroleum Institute	"Industry and Government Changes Post Macondo—A Presentation by Executive Director, Center for Offshore Safety, Charlie Williams, to Oil Spill Commission Action," API.org, April 2012. www.api.org.

Celia Ampek	"EPA Regulations Stifle Economy, Oil and Gas Industry Reps Testify," NewsOK.com, July 14, 2012. http://newsok.com.
Associated Press	"Big Oil Plans Rapid Response to Future Spills," AL.com, July 21, 2010. http://blog.al.com.
Carolyn Barry	"Slick Death: Oil-Spill Treatment Kills Coral," *Science News*, vol. 172, August 4, 2007.
Christopher Beddor et al.	"Securing America's Future: Enhancing Our National Security by Reducing Oil Dependence and Environmental Damage," Center for American Progress, August 2009. www.americanprogress.org.
Philip Bump	"Today, Congress Will Hear About How Chickens Are Impairing the Oil Industry," Grist, July 13, 2012. http://grist.org.
Mark Clayton	"Lawmakers Slam Big Oil Executives on Spill Preparedness," *Christian Science Monitor*, June 15, 2010. www.csmonitor.com.
CNN	"Oil Disaster By the Numbers," CNN.com, July 1, 2010. www.cnn.com.
Geoff Dembicki	"Gulf Disaster Raises Alarms About Alberta to Texas Pipeline," *The Tyee*, June 21, 2010. http://thetyee.ca.

Lou Dolinar	"Our Real Gulf Disaster," *National Review*, vol. 62, no. 16, August 30, 2010.
Scott Eustis	"Science of the Spill: Two Years Later, the Gulf Is Fuel-Injected," Gulf Restoration Network, April 17, 2012. http://healthygulf.org.
Humberto Fontova	"Offshore Oil Drilling: An Environmental Bonanza," *American Thinker*, April 28, 2009. www.americanthinker.com.
Henry Fountain	"Advances in Oil Spill Cleanup Lag Since Valdez," *New York Times*, June 24, 2010.
Eric Fox	"Bubbling Crude: America's Top 6 Oil-producing States," MSNBC.com, June 8, 2011. www.msnbc.msn.com.
Thomas Friedman	"Addicted to Oil," *New York Times*, June 22, 2008. www.nytimes.com.
Jack Gerard	"Committed to Offshore Safety," *National Journal*, May 1, 2012. http://energy.nationaljournal.com.
Gloria Gonzalez	"Oil Companies Still Hiding the True Risks of Deepwater Drilling from Investors," OilPrice.com, August 5, 2012. http://oilprice.com.
Jeremy Hance	"Who's to Blame for the Oil Spill?" Mongabay.com, May 4, 2010. www.mongabay.com.

Andrea Harden-Donahue	"Alberta Oil Well Rupture Caused by Fracking?" Council of Canadians, January 17, 2012. http://canadians.org/blog.
Steve Harvey	"California's Legendary Oil Spill," *Los Angeles Times*, June 13, 2010.
Jack Hays and T. Scott Martin	"Don't Stifle Economic Recovery with New Layers of Regulation for Energy Development," Common Sense Policy Roundtable, 2012. http://commonsensepolicyround table.com.
Christopher Helman	"Meet the Oil Shale Eighty Times Bigger than the Bakken," *Forbes*, June 4, 2012.
Christopher Helman	"Two Years After the Spill, BP Has a Secret: It's Booming," *Forbes*, May 7, 2012.
Andrew Holland	"Gulf Oil Spill: Two Years Later, Safety Lessons Ignored," *Christian Science Monitor*, April 20, 2012.
Inside Climate News	"Oil Industry Unprepared to Clean Up Spill in Harsh Arctic Climate, Report Warns," InsideClimate News, November 11, 2010. http://inside climatenews.org.

Dahr Jamail	"BP Blamed for Ongoing Health Problems: Gulf Coast Residents and Clean Up Workers Have Found Chemicals Present in BP's Oil in Their Own Bloodstreams," Al Jazeera, April 20, 2012. www.aljazeera.com.
Rick Jervis	"Judge OKs $4B BP Oil Spill Criminal Settlement," *USA Today*, January 29, 2013.
Bailey Johnson	"'Dirty Bathtub' Buried Oil from BP Spill," CBS News, January 28, 2013. www.cbsnews.com.
Patrik Jonsson	"Transocean Deepwater Horizon Oil Rig Explosion Shows New Risks," *Christian Science Monitor*, April 21, 2010.
Antonia Juhasz	"Two Years After the BP Spill, a Hidden Health Crisis Festers," *The Nation*, May 7, 2012. www.thenation.com.
Adam Kingsmith	"Enbridge's Great Northern Gateway Debacle," *The International*, September 28, 2012. www.theinternational.org.
Charles Krauthammer	"A Disaster with Many Fathers," *Washington Post*, May 28, 2010.
Michael Kunzelman	"Judge Approves Transocean's $1B Spill Settlement," ABCNews.com, February 19, 2013. http://abcnews.go.com.

Dave Levitan   "Montana Oil Spill Illustrates Climate-Related Risks to Pipelines, Experts Say," ClimateCentral.org, July 8, 2011. www.climatecentral.org.

Abrahm Lustgarten   "A Stain That Won't Wash Away," *New York Times*, April 19, 2012.

Joseph R. Mason   "The Economic Cost of a Moratorium on Offshore Oil and Gas Exploration to the Gulf Region," Save U.S. Energy Jobs, July 2010. www.saveusenergyjobs.com.

James McKinley Jr. and Leslie Kaufman   "New Ways to Drill, Old Methods for Cleanup," *New York Times*, May 10, 2010.

Russell McLendon   "Offshore Drilling: Low Bills vs. Big Spills," Mother Nature Network, May 27, 2010. www.mnn.com.

NBC News Wire Services   "Environmental Risk of Drilling in Arctic Too High, CEO of Oil Giant Total Says," *Worldnews*, September 26, 2012. www.worldnews.nbcnews.com.

New York Times   "The Big Spill, Two Years Later," April 17, 2012. www.nytimes.com.

Riki Ott   "Hide and Leak: BP's Cleanup Is More Like a Cover Up—Holding the Company Accountable Will Require Digging for the Truth," *Earth Island Journal*, vol. 25, no. 3, Autumn 2010.

Paul Parfomak et al.	"Keystone XL Pipeline Project: Key Issues," Congressional Research Service/Federation of American Scientists, May 7, 2013. www.fas.org.
Michael Pearson	"Judge OKs Transocean Agreement on Civil Penalties," CNN.com, February 19, 2013. www.cnn.com.
Thomas Pyle	"Approving Keystone XL Pipeline Would Create Jobs and Lower Gas Prices," *US News & World Report*, July 27, 2011.
Orpheus Reed	"'Damage Control' and the Real Damage Done: Gulf Oil Disaster Is NOT Over," *Revolution*, vol. 209, August 15, 2010.
Campbell Robertson and Clifford Krauss	"Gulf Spill Is the Largest of Its Kind, Scientists Say," *New York Times*, August 2, 2010. www.nytimes.com.
David Sassoon	"Lessons from the DilBit Disaster," InsideClimate News, August 21, 2012. http://insideclimatenews.org.
Mark Schleifstein	"Oil Spill Trial Begins for BP, Transocean, Other Companies," *The Times-Picayune*, February 25, 2013. www.nola.com.
Jim Snyder	"Shell Arctic Setback Shows Risks, Environmentalists Say," *Bloomberg Business Week*, September 18, 2012. www.businessweek.com.

US Environmental Protection Agency	"Oil Spills," EPA.gov, 2012. www.epa.gov.
Grace Visconti	"Keystone XL Pipeline (Parts 1–3)," *Digital Journal*, September 7, 2011. http://digitaljournal.com.
Bryan Walsh	"Gulf Oil Spill: Scientists Escalate Environmental Warnings," *Time*, May 19, 2010.
Bryan Walsh	"Remembering the Lessons of the Exxon Valdez," *Time*, March 24, 2009.
Ronald D. White	"Economic Damage in Gulf of Mexico Oil Spill Could Be Permanent," *Los Angeles Times*, May 6, 2010.
World Wildlife Federation	"20 Years On, Arctic Unprepared for Another Exxon Valdez," WWF, March 2009. http://wwf.panda.org.

Index

H

Habitat sensitivity factor, 52
Hahn, Robert, 50–52
Harper, Stephen, 58
Hashim, David, 99–100
Hayek, Friedrich, 137
Hayward, Tony, 79
Heiman, Marilyn, 95, 97
Helman, Christopher, 54–62
Henry, Simon, 101
Heritage Foundation, 127
Hertsgaard, Mark, 66–79
Horsman, Paul, 41
Hurlburt, Adam, 104–110
Hydraulic fracturing (fracking).
  See Fracking
Hydrocarbon concerns, 29–30,
  104, 122
Hypothermia concerns in wildlife,
  23, 24

I

Iles, Derric, 106–107
Industrial revolution, 63
Institute of Social and Economic
  Research, 133
Institute on Water Resources Law
  and Policy, 71
International Tanker Owners Pol-
  lution Federation Limited, 24
Iran, 61–62
Israel, 62

J

Jackson, Lisa, 72
Jeffers, Alan, 90
Jones, Jeffrey M., 44–48

Journal of Petroleum Technology,
  100

K

Kahn, Chris, 89–91
Kalamazoo River spill, 38, 55,
  122–123
Kearl development, 57
Keller, Luke, 77–78
Keystone XL Pipeline
  approval for, 44, 46–47
  construction of, 17
  controversy over, 54
  diluted bitumen transport,
    119–120, 123, 126
  transporting DilBit through,
    36–38
Kilburn, Kaye H., 67
Kotlikoff, Laurence, 137
Kuwait, 24, 40–42

L

Lautenberg, Frank R., 37
Levitt, Tom, 92–94
Limbaugh, Rush, 70
Loris, Nicolas D., 127–131
Louisiana Environmental Action
  Network (LEAN), 71, 77
Louisiana Light Sweet crude, 60,
  68
Louisiana Shrimp Association, 74
Louisiana State University, 134

M

MacArthur Foundation, 71
Magnets to clean oil spills, 92–94
Marine animal concerns, 22–23